Michael Waddle

Mission and Dialogue

Mission and Dialogue

PROCLAIMING THE GOSPEL

AFRESH IN EVERY AGE

✳

Michael Nazir-Ali

First published in Great Britain 1995
Society for Promoting Christian Knowledge
Holy Trinity Church
Marylebone Road
London NW1 4DU

British Library Cataloguing-in-Publication Data
A catalogue record for this book is available from the British Library

ISBN 0-281-04810-x

Typeset by Wilmaset Ltd, Birkenhead, Wirral
Printed in Great Britain by
Redwood Books, Trowbridge, Wiltshire

Contents

Acknowledgements

Chapter 1 was first published under the title 'The Christian faith: context, communication and content', chapter 11 of Eden and Wells (eds.), *The Gospel in the Modern World* © IVP 1991. Used by permission.

Chapter 2 was previously published under the title 'Culture, Conversation and Conversion: Some Priorities in Contemporary Mission', chapter 3 of V. Samuel and C. M. N. Sugden (eds.), *AD 2000 and Beyond: A Mission Agenda* (Oxford, Regnum Books, 1991). Copyright is retained by the author.

Chapter 4 was previously published as an article in the *CMS Newsletter*, July/August 1993, Number 513.

Chapter 6 was previously published as two articles in the *CMS Newsletter*, May/June 1992, Number 506 and July/August 1992, Number 507.

Chapter 7 was first published under the same title, chapter 7 of D. Cohn-Sherbok (ed.), *Many Mansions* (Bellew Publishing Company, 1992). Used by permission.

Chapter 9 was first published under the title 'A Christian View of Prayer and Spirituality in Muslim Thought', chapter 11 of D. A. Carson (ed.), *Teach Us to Pray* (Exeter, Paternoster Press, 1990).

Chapter 11 was previously published as an article in the *CMS Newsletter*, July/August 1991, Number 501.

Chapter 13 was previously published as an article in the *CMS Newsletter*, January/February 1993, Number 510.

Biblical quotations are mostly taken from *The Revised Standard Version of the Bible* (RSV), copyright 1946, 1952, 1971 by the Division of Christian Education of the National Council of the Churches of Christ in the USA.

The version of the Qu'rān used is that of A. Yusuf ᶜAli, *The Holy Qu'rān: Text, Translation and Commentary* (Leicester, Islamic Foundation, 1975).

Preface

The Church is called to proclaim the gospel afresh in every age. This means, first of all, to be aware of the *original* contexts in which God spoke and acted among his people and in the wider world. It involves a close study of the languages, cultures, and history of the peoples to whom God first revealed himself. It also involves making a distinction between divine revelation and the vehicles in which it has been conveyed. This is difficult to do as languages naturally reflect the cultures in which they arise and develop, and the languages in which God's revelation is recorded are no exception. It is important, nevertheless, to distinguish between such fundamental acts of God as the Exodus from Egypt or the settlement in Canaan and the particular ways in which they have been presented and interpreted in the Hebrew Bible. This may also be true of the New Testament's attempts to work out the moral implications of the gospel in terms of acceptable behaviour in the Graeco-Roman world of the first century AD.

Second, the Church is called to live out and to share her experience of God as just, powerful, and loving in the midst of a variety of cultures, world-views, and religious beliefs. To be able to do this effectively, the Church needs to understand *each* of the contexts in which she has been placed. This involves a deep commitment to dialogue with people representing every aspect of life; whether it is the sciences, the arts, politics, or the social sciences. In particular, there should be a commitment to dialogue with those of other faiths.

Such dialogue will be an occasion for much listening but also for sensitive witness to God's work in Jesus Christ. It can almost be said that dialogue is both a necessary preparation and an occasion for the proclamation of the gospel.

It is not the *only* occasion, of course. Christ is also made known when we serve our fellow human beings in his name. He is made known through drama, poetry, music, and art. He is made known through preaching, and in the Church's sacraments. However it is that we make him known, the horizon of God's revelation in its original contexts will need to be related to the horizon of the rapidly changing contexts of today's world. What follows is an attempt to do this, keeping particularly in mind the universality of the gospel, which allows it to be translated not only into every language but into every culture and world-view. Specific issues which are addressed include understanding the uniqueness of Christ in a plural world, relating the gospel to human development and transformation, relations with people of other faiths, and the need for unity for the sake of mission.

> Take not, oh Lord, our literal sense. Lord, in thy great
> Unbroken speech our limping metaphor translate.

C. S. Lewis

Michael Nazir-Ali

— PART ONE —

Mission

— 1 —
The Christian Faith: God's Love for the World

✳

To speak of the content of faith, without also mentioning the context in which such a faith is set, as well as ways in which it is to be communicated, would be rather like a medieval schoolman asked to speak on substance without reference to accidents. Medieval school-men, of course, were capable of doing so. I cannot pretend to such facility myself, and it is not possible to talk about the content of our faith without also talking about the work, the witness, and the worship where this faith is expressed.

— The Context of Faith —

The form of divine revelation is given to us in particular contexts, and is not given apart from those contexts. The normative record of divine revelation in the Bible cannot be encountered precisely as revelation until the worshipping and witnessing and reading community has come to grips with the contexts of the Bible. It is necessary for us to come to grips with the language, with the thought forms, with the idiom, and with the culture of the periods in which the biblical revelation was first given. But the horizon of the Bible – its culture and idiom – has to be related to the contemporary world, to *our* horizon. Our context too is therefore exceedingly important if we are to encounter the revelation of God in a living and immediate way.

Different communities, individuals, and groups of people find that they have particular affinities with particular themes of the Bible. Biblical scholars nowadays call them trajectories. Our particular upbringing, culture, maybe even our language, equip us to have a special insight about a particular theme, a trajectory, in the Bible.[1] The renewal that the Church has experienced through the reading of the Bible in context cannot be overemphasized. In all sorts of ways, all kinds of Christians, with all sorts of commitment, have come to a

3

realization that when they allow the Bible to interact with their context, then new, strange, and wonderful things happen. Some people have come to the conclusion that the ways in which the Bible speaks of the experience of the Holy Spirit almost as an invasive experience is something that speaks to them. They find that the prophets in the Old Testament are led to do strange and wonderful things for God because of this kind of experience of the Holy Spirit. They find this confirmed, of course, in the experience of the early church at Pentecost.[2] They discover that in their situation this is the way that God is speaking to them. They can see that this kind of experience of the Holy Spirit is right for themselves and their community.

This discovery has happened across a wide range of Christian traditions. I remember visiting an old church in the middle of Manila *intra muros*. It was very depressing to see this church, because it was traditional Roman Catholicism at its worst. Immediately afterwards I was taken to the Roman Catholic cathedral in Manila. There I found that the charismatic movement in the Roman Catholic Church had taken hold of the congregation and the clergy. It was nothing like the other church at all.

There are others who have found the passionate concern for justice in the prophets something that has spoken to *them* in their situation. These people have found that the God who is just, and who justifies sinners, is also a God who demands justice in his world. Again this phenomenon has occurred over an extremely wide range of Christian commitment and tradition. We cannot say that it is only radicals in Latin America who are into this kind of thing, because it makes an impact on people in strange ways and at different times. A recent testimony to this was given to me by a friend of mine who is a Jewish Rabbi, and teaches at the University of Kent in Canterbury. He has written a book called *On Earth as it is in Heaven*, on how liberation theology in Latin America has alerted him to his own prophetic tradition, and made it come alive for him.[3] There are yet others who find the theme of liberation in the Bible, the Exodus narrative for example, something that speaks to them. The American blacks in the nineteenth century, groaning under the burden of slavery, found that the Exodus narrative was something with which they could identify. So it is not surprising that many 'Negro spirituals' are about the Exodus. Today, the modern 'slaves' of urban Latin America and Asia also identify with the Exodus narrative, as a way of release from the captivity that notions of development forced upon them have brought about in urban areas of the two-thirds world.

4

Now, for each context, the insight a community has into the Scripture is ultimately valuable for that community and yet at the same time for all of us, as we need each other. Private judgement, the Reformers' recovery of the insight that the reading of the Bible can speak in an immediate way to us, is something that we must not lose. I do not always agree with Dr David Samuel, until recently Director of Church Society. But he speaks of the immediate, felt authority of Scripture. This is something that we need to relearn. There is a place for private judgement. There is a way in which Scripture makes itself felt in an authoritative way for us as individuals, as communities, as churches. That doctrine of private judgement, however, has to be complemented by a doctrine of the Church. In other words, we need to complement and supplement each other's insights. So there is a sense in which no particular context can dictate to others about what is ultimate in the Christian scheme of things.

The Content of Our Faith

GOD'S LOVE AND THE TRINITY

Now I must apply Ockham's razor to the substantial matter before us, the content of our faith.

'God is love' is about the briefest proposition there is in the Bible. This proposition is not just about the relation of the Godhead to us. It also concerns the mystery of the Godhead itself. It is about the heart of the Godhead, the internal relationships within the Godhead. The Father loves the Son, the Son loves the Father. St Augustine, in a famous remark that has never been forgotten, said that the Holy Spirit was the *vinculum amoris*, the bond of love between the Father and the Son. Of course, the Holy Spirit is, and has always been, understood by the Church and in the Bible as communal, as the communion not only between the Father and the Son, but between God and human beings, and among believers. Bishop John Taylor, in his wonderful book *The Go-between God*, reminds us that when we say the Grace, as we so often do, we say: 'The grace of our Lord Jesus Christ, the love of God and the fellowship (or the communion) of the Holy Spirit.'[4] Augustine has been criticized by some who have asked whether his understanding does not reduce the Holy Spirit, doing injustice to the Spirit's personality and reducing the Spirit to a relation. Bishop John sees the Holy Spirit not so much as a bond but as a medium in which love can take place – the love that the Father has for the Son, and the Son has for the Father, that God has for human beings, and the love that they can have for each other.[5]

But whether as bond or as medium, does this not to some extent depersonalize the Holy Spirit?

Augustine's reference to the Holy Spirit as the bond of love is not all that he has said about the Holy Spirit, of course. In his work on the Trinity, and in the latter part of his *Confessions*, he elaborates what has come to be known as the psychological analogy. In this analogy, Augustine compares the human self with God the Father, the fount, the source of the Godhead. He compares the human mind with God the Eternal Word, and the human will (or the human capacity of love) with the Holy Spirit. Augustine insists again and again that the three persons of the Godhead, the Father, the Word, and the Spirit, are in the most intimate union with each other. For this reason he is very reluctant to refer to them even as persons. He says that he uses the word 'person' because there is no better word to hand. Augustine is very strong on what came to be called the doctrine of co-inherence. According to this, the persons of the blessed Trinity share in each other's qualities, and in each other's work, so what can be said of the Son can also be said of the Father, and what is said of the Son can also be said of the Holy Spirit, and so on. The important point is that this doctrine of co-inherence for Augustine only makes sense because he is willing to use the analogy of a single person for the Godhead.[6]

The Western Christian tradition in its thinking on the Trinity has always begun with the oneness of God, and then gone on to consider how there could be diversity in this unity. The Christian Orient agrees with the West on this point. (By the Orient, I mean those churches that did not accept the Council of Chalcedon, i.e., the Coptic, Ethiopian, Syrian, Indian, and Armenian Churches.) But the East – the Greek and the Russian East – have always begun with the plurality of experience of God, with God experienced as Father, Son, and Holy Spirit, and then gone on to ask the question: 'How can these three be one?' The most orthodox expositions of the Eastern tradition safeguard the oneness of God by laying heavy emphasis on co-inherence. But this is very difficult to do. So, quite often in the East, the danger is of slipping into a kind of tritheism. I believe that the Western theological tradition has been faithful to the biblical faith in beginning with the oneness of God, and then going on to ask how diversities are possible within that divine unity, a unity which is given, and which the Church has inherited from Israel.

There is a lamentable tendency these days to use the doctrine of the Trinity, and particularly the social analogy as it was used by the Eastern Fathers, to build all sorts of houses of cards. So the cause of ecumenism is commended because there is diversity, they say, in the unity of the

Godhead; diversity in the community is commended because of an alleged diversity in the Godhead. I have even heard the family being described in terms that were analogically taken from the doctrine of the Trinity! Now as someone who has lived and worked in a Muslim culture, I have found this quite disturbing, because most of our apologetic work for Muslims has been to show precisely that we do not believe in three Gods, but that we believe in one God who is nevertheless experienced in these diverse ways.[7]

The love of God is creative and boundless. It is not limited, therefore, to the Godhead itself, but it spills over into creation. We see the Trinity active in creation. The Father wills creation; the pattern, the design, and the order of creation reflects God the Word, the Logos; and the power, the energy, and the personality which we encounter in creation all reflect God the Holy Spirit. We must remember, however, that because of co-inherence, what is said of the one can also be said of the others.

God's Love and Creation

If science is possible because the human mind encounters design, pattern and order in the world, then there is a way in which we can develop an apologetic to the scientific community properly based on a theology of the Word. There are, of course, scientists who are now beginning to see that design and pattern are not just about breaking things down into their constituent parts. There is such a thing as end, as final cause, which determines what a thing is. They are now talking, for example, about the so-called anthropic principle, according to which the evolution of the universe, and the wonderful checks and balances that we encounter in this world, can only make sense if we posit a human being at the end of the process. That is, the process can be seen from this end as leading up to the emergence of rational, self-conscious, moral, and spiritual beings. Now, though scientists are not drawing any theological conclusions from this, I think we are free to do so.[8] The order, design, and pattern of the universe reflect God the Word. If science has most to do with God the Word, then perhaps it is poetry that has most to do with God the Holy Spirit as encountered in the universe. It is our response to the Holy Spirit that makes poetry possible.

From creation in general we get to what is perhaps the climax of creation – the creation of human beings. It is here that we find divine love bringing about the creation of a being able to respond in love. But to be able to respond in love, one must be free; there can be no coercion in love. The freedom of the human being is involved in the eliciting of this free response of love. So human beings are created *posse non peccare*, with the possibility of not sinning, but that implies *posse peccare*, the possibility of sinning. Love cannot be something that is compelled. We know as a matter of fact that human beings have refused to respond to the invitation of divine love, so the *posse peccare*, the possibility of sinning, has in fact become actual. Nor is it episodic, it is not something that has happened once for all. It is something that has happened, happened again, and continues to happen; it is, in short, endemic. It has become endemic to the human situation. Since the coming of sin, the human situation is one of *non posse non peccare*, the inability not to sin. There is no way in which human beings cannot sin. It is here that in the divine revelation we find a wholly new trajectory introduced, if you want to use that fashionable word, and so divine love is now not only about creation, but about redemption. It is very easy to separate, rather artificially, creation and redemption. There is, however, a very real sense in which a new sort of discussion begins in the Bible after the introduction of the theme of human sin.

God's Love and Salvation History

The history of redemption has been more often termed 'Salvation History'. Let us begin with the Exodus, and God's choice of a people for himself. Why did he choose them? They were not a beautiful people, wealthy and powerful. They were in fact exploited, oppressed, and rejected slaves in a very large imperial context. I'm not an Old Testament scholar, and I stand to be corrected, but I believe that the *Habiru* people, of whom the Israelites were a part, were a despised social group in ancient Middle-Eastern societies.[9] Why did God choose them? The answer is found in the Bible itself. He chose them so that they could be a light to lighten the nations (Isa. 49.6; 62.6; Luke 2.32). Even in the particular choice of a specific people, God's purposes were universal.

While the perception of the Israelites during the ages, from time to time, was rather less than perfect about why they had been chosen, that cannot limit us from seeing why they were chosen, and what the purpose of God was. Sometimes the Israelites thought that they had been chosen to bring judgement on the world. I think there is an element of truth in this. There was a kind of judgement that the Israelites brought to the nations of Canaan, for example, where the city states were organized around an axis of priests and kings. The advent of the Israelites, the tribes of Yahweh as they have been called, destroyed the system in Canaan, and introduced what is widely recognized by sociologists of the period as social and political egalitarianism. One sociologist of the period has said that Yahwism can be defined as a function of social and political egalitarianism at that time in Canaan.[10] John Goldingay, in a marvellous response, has pointed out that one could also say that social and political egalitarianism in Canaan at that time was a function of Yahwism![11]

Very quickly the Israelites, and particularly the prophets among them, began to see that if their God was universal, if he was truly the God of the whole world and of all human beings, then their choice must mean something in the context of the history of the world. They could not reduce Yahweh to being a tribal God. This is why you see, scattered throughout the Old Testament, different models of understanding what can be called biblical universalism. You find, for example, the great visions in Isaiah and Micah, where Israel is shown as understanding its cultic focus, Zion, as the centre of the world. All the different nations stream there. We are all familiar with those wonderful prophecies we read at Christmas-time. But the same prophets very often saw that this marvellously centripetal view of history was not adequate. They began to see that God was at work in the nations where they were. So we have the eschatological visions in Isaiah 19, where Israel sees that a time will come when Egypt will be the people of God, Assyria will be the work of his hands, and Israel will be his heritage. Now some people say: 'All that's in the future. You cannot build too much on it.'[12] In the Bible itself, however, we have evidence that the biblical writers were beginning to see that the history of God's work among the nations goes back to their very origin. It is not just an eschatological vision for the future. So we have the recognition that the God who brought the Israelites out of Egypt is also the God who has made the Ethiopians a nation, who has brought the Philistines out from Crete, and the Syrians from Kir (Amos 9.7). When the prophet Malachi is rebuking the Israelites for offering polluted sacrifices to Yahweh, he acknowledges at the same time that there are sincere seekers after truth and, perhaps, even sincere worshippers in the nations round about (Mal. 1). This does not mean, however, that the prophet necessarily endorses the *cults* of these nations.

Already in the Old Testament, then, we have a situation of many salvation histories, where God is working among people, cultures, and groups. Now this in no way reduces the need for having normative salvation history, because, if we do not have a touchstone, a paradigm, how are we to determine what is authentically salvation history in a particular people? In India, or in Pakistan, or among pagan Europeans, or whoever it may be, how are we to determine, without a paradigm, what it is that authentically prepares them for the gospel, or encounter with God? Salvation history in the Bible is our touchstone for determining whether it is the dominant religious tradition of a people that prepares them for encounter with God, or whether it is a counter-religious movement. In many cases the dominant religious tradition is merely oppressive. In such cases, is it the forces for social and political change that are the salvation histories of these people? We cannot determine these matters without reference to a paradigm. This is illustrated by Oscar Cullmann's diagram which incorporates the shape of the St Andrew's cross cutting across the biblical line of time.[13] Salvation history begins with Israel, narrows down to Christ, and then goes out again to the world. Christ paradoxically is the most particular act, where God's choice is concerned, and yet the most universal – because he includes all that is to come. I have always been very impressed with Karl Barth's exegesis of Ephesians 1.4, where it talks about God having chosen us in Christ before the foundation of the world. Barth's point is that it is only Christ who has been chosen eternally; all of us are chosen by virtue of our incorporation in Christ. In this way Barth saves both the doctrine of predestination and also that of human choice.[14]

GOD'S LOVE AND THE ATONEMENT

Salvation history comes to its climax in the incarnation of God the Word. Ever since the publication of Lux Mundi, Anglicans have been rather good at taking seriously the doctrine of the incarnation.[15] Sometimes I have wondered whether this is not because the English Anglican tradition finds itself incarnate in the parochial system! There is no choice in the matter. The church has to be present in the inner cities, in the villages, and in the suburbs. It is easy, therefore, to take incarnation seriously. The Anglican tradition is deeply committed to it and, at the same time, is rightly suspicious of hit-and-run evangelism and pastoral work. But has Anglican incarnation been kenotic? At about the same time as Lux Mundi was being written, Bishop Gore and others were also developing their views on kenosis, on the self-emptying of the divine Word in his human condition.[16] While we can say of Anglicanism that it can be incarnational in its structure and its forms, we have to ask how far this incarnation is kenotic.

The incarnation, and kenosis, which is a giving-up, an emptying ('our Lord Jesus Christ, . . . though he was rich, yet for your sakes he became poor', 2 Cor. 8.9), bring us all to alertness about sacrifice. Most people in the West these days know very little about sacrifice. They may talk about it and may even preach about it, but how many have actually seen a sacrifice? Every year in Pakistan we are all treated to this spectacle, and I cannot pretend that it is a pleasant occasion, but you do see sacrifice. I have begun to realize how deeply rooted the biblical writers are in the metaphors of sacrifice because of their familiarity with the Hebraic system of sacrifice. Kenosis brings us to sacrifice, to atonement, which, of course, means at-one-ment, reconciliation. I would not limit atonement simply to the cross. It is part and parcel of, and integrally related to, the incarnation itself. The whole of the incarnation may be understood as sacrifice, and as atonement; the whole of it has to be understood as reconciliation. Again and again I find that all kinds of people are reconciled to God because of something in the life of Christ. It may be his teaching. For Muslims very often it is his healing power. It may be an appreciation of the cross and the resurrection. But often it is not just one thing. The cross may rightly be regarded as the climax to this work of atonement, reconciliation and sacrifice, but it cannot be separated from the rest of Christ's life.

The atonement is objective because God has set forth a way of reconciliation in Christ. It is objective because, in Christ, God has begun a new humanity. The beginnings of a new humanity occur in this reconciling, atoning, sacrificial life and death. It has a representative character because, if our situation is truly *non posse non peccare*, the inability not to sin, then we need rescue; a way has to be set forth to rescue us from our predicament. There is a subjective element also about the atonement because, unless we respond to what God has set forth, the atonement remains meaningless to us. It is not, of course, meaningless in itself. We do not know what the atonement means for those who do not respond to it; only God in his wisdom knows. But for us it must remain meaningless unless we decide to follow Christ, to follow the way of the cross, to be incorporated into this new thing, into this new life. It remains meaningless unless we decide to forgo our solidarity in the sin of the old Adam, and to forge our solidarity in this new life, this new Adam – the last Adam as the New Testament sometimes calls him (1 Cor. 15.45).

From the very earliest times, both Scripture and the Fathers have strongly denied that the incarnation could be merely a semblance. I've been re-reading recently the Epistles of Ignatius, which he wrote on his way to martyrdom. I have been struck how often Ignatius insists that Christ has truly come in the flesh, and truly died in the flesh.

Docetism is not an option for Christians; the incarnation was not a semblance. The resurrection of Jesus Christ from the dead is part of the apparatus of the incarnation. I find it very difficult to believe people who claim to have a strong doctrine of the incarnation, but have a weak doctrine of the resurrection. If docetism is not possible at one end, it is not possible at the other. Now, of course, the fledgling Christian community was called with reason 'the Easter community' because it was the Easter faith that had brought them together. It was Pentecost, however, the coming of the Holy Spirit, that empowered them for their mission to the world. So we are back to the first verses of the book of Genesis, the Spirit creatively brooding over the void and bringing creation out of nothing. It is the same with the creation of the Church. Pentecost makes the Church out of nothing, as it were, and sends the Church out for mission, for communicating the Faith to those whom God has created and wants to save.

'Tis Love, 'tis Love! Thou diedst for me!
I hear Thy whisper in my heart;
The morning breaks, the shadows flee,
Pure, universal Love Thou art;
To me, to all, Thy mercies move:
Thy nature and thy name is Love.[17]

— 2 —
The Universal Gospel

✳

—— *Mobility and Cultural Change* ——

Some years ago, we moved from a Victorian vicarage in Oxford to a rather typical house on the outskirts of London, and culture, quite naturally, was much on my mind as we made the change. I have been spotting all sorts of cultural differences. The use of the motor car, for example; how often people use the motor car in the suburbs of London, while in Oxford people still either walk or use the bicycle. Again, it is interesting to observe how people do their shopping, what sorts of things they buy and the kinds of shops they patronize. Even the intercessions in the parish church; how people pray and what they pray for are very different in different places.

A colleague of mine was a presbyter in this country and then went to Lahore to be a presbyter there. The transition from this land to Lahore was wonderfully smooth, the family enjoyed the change of culture and the children settled in quickly. And then he was appointed to a position here and the move from Lahore to London was rather less smooth. The family did not particularly want to move to London, and while they live in a desirable part of London, there have been cultural obstacles to adjustment. They often reflect that while adjustment to Lahore produced only a few problems, adjustment to London presented serious problems for them as a family.

Culture, of course, and cultural change are very important for the modern world because there is so much mobility. People are being urged all the time these days to get on their bicycles and go and find work. I am told that there is an express train that leaves London every Friday for Liverpool which is called the 'Tebbit Express'[1] because it carries all sorts of young people who have not been able to find work in Liverpool, who have gone to London, and who go home at the weekend. So mobility and cultural change are part of our daily experience.

—— *Destruction of Cultures* ——

One aspect of culture has to do with our consciousness that *our* culture is special. There are perfectly acceptable and healthy manifestations of this feeling. Despite all evidence to the contrary, I still firmly believe that the Pakistan cricket team is the best in the world. I am open to correction, but I feel that this is not very pathological. On the other hand, there are dangers in thinking of our culture as so special that it leads to discrimination against people of other cultures and even to destruction of other cultures.

In the nineteenth century, dominant cultures destroyed other cultures that did not match their expectations of what human culture ought to be. Compare, for example, how the imperial powers dealt with Asian cultures, on the one hand, and African cultures on the other. Asian cultures had analogues to the European experience: books, organized religion, and a hierarchically ordered society. These cultures were allowed to survive, and a great deal of scholarship was carried on by people from the dominant cultures *vis-à-vis* the Asian. But African cultures, and even more so perhaps Aboriginal cultures in South America and in Australia (New Zealand is an exception), were destroyed or regarded as demonic because these did not have analogues to the European experience. We are only just emerging from that period.

The Christian Church was implicated in at least some of these experiments, and this is a matter for repentance. Some outstanding people were not implicated, and tried to sustain and nurture traditional cultures. We really owe our modern understanding of culture to the emergence of the discipline of social and cultural anthropology, the work of people like Raymond Firth, the New Zealand anthropologist, and Margaret Mead. People began to realize the value of traditional cultures and began to see that the study of them had value for our understanding of our own culture, even if that culture were rapidly changing.

—— *Israel* ——

The nation of Israel regarded itself as special. This is not remarkable, because every culture does this. But Israel's consciousness of being special was tied up with their experience of *Yahweh* as their God who had liberated them from slavery and oppression. Different tribes and nations in the Middle East in those days also regarded themselves as being in a special relationship with *their* god. What made Israel distinctive was the belief that they were special, chosen, *and* had been liberated in a special way. Alongside went the belief that their God, Yahweh, was not just their God but was the Lord of the universe, and God of all people. So the logic of election was and is always held together in the Scriptures with the logic of universality.[2]

Israel did forget sometimes that election and universality had to be held together, and felt that they had been chosen because there was something special about them. They forgot the reason why they were chosen – to be a witness to the nations, to be a light to lighten the gentiles as we sing in the *Song of Simeon*. Sometimes they felt that the universal significance of Yahweh was to allow Israel to wipe out all the other nations, or to achieve dominance over them, or to enslave them, to extend the frontiers of their empire. All these things have contemporary significance. But then at other times, perhaps in a kindlier mood, they thought that God, if he is the God of all people, must have a purpose for these people which must really be that they should become exactly like Israel. The great passages in the prophets, in Micah and the early part of Isaiah, mentioned earlier, speak of the nations converging onto Mount Zion. Zion is the centre of the world, *the* culture, and everybody else comes to it and partakes of its benefits. Their model of mission was that everyone else should be like them. This model of mission has been pursued at other times when grass skirts were taken off people, and trousers put on them in the name of Christian mission! Havelock Ellis, not a great friend of the Christian Church, said once that the white man arrived in the Pacific with the Bible, trousers, and syphilis. That is to say, the Gospel came tied up with all sorts of cultural baggage.

—— *Universality in the Old Testament* ——

We have also seen, however, that at its best, the witness of the Old Testament is more than this because in Isaiah, chapter 19, one begins to get the realization that the God of Israel who has so miraculously saved Israel and made it a nation, is also at work in other people, even among the enemies of Israel. And so the great eschatological vision of Isaiah 19 ends with God saying 'In that day Israel will be the third with Egypt and Assyria, a blessing in the midst of the earth, whom the Lord of hosts has blessed, saying, "Blessed be Egypt my people, and Assyria the work of my hands, and Israel my heritage" ' (Isa. 19. 24–25). This is an aspect of biblical universalism: God is at work among all peoples, in all cultures. It was a historian who said 'all civilizations are at an equal distance from God'.

In Malachi we have that amazing section in chapter 1 to which few commentators devote enough attention. God is indicting and condemning the people of Israel for offering him polluted sacrifices, and then he says, 'For from the rising of the sun to its setting my name is great among the nations, and in every place incense is offered to my name, and a pure offering; for my name is great among the nations, says the Lord of hosts' (Mal. 1. 11–12, the tense is flexible throughout). Some commentators, to make a doctrinal point, hold that the meaning is future. But I think their case is unconvincing, as it does not easily cohere with the logic of the passage. What is even more remarkable is that the word used here for a pure offering, the word *tahor*, is not usually used in the Old Testament for an unblemished sacrifice; that word is *tamim*. *Tahor* in Hebrew and its Arabic cognates often means moral rather than merely ritual purity.[3] An acknowledgement that there may have been sincere seekers after truth, and even worshippers of the true God among the nations at this time of Israel's apostasy is significant even if it does not endorse the religious systems of these nations.[4]

Towards the end of the book of Amos, in a dialogue between God and Israel, God says to Israel, 'Are you not like the Ethiopians to me, O people of Israel? Did I not bring up Israel from the land of Egypt, and the Philistines from Caphtor and the Syrians from Kir?' So even the Exodus, that foundation event in the life of Israel, is not unique in the sense that some have understood it to be, because God is working among the Philistines and the Ethiopians and the Syrians in the same way.

Universality in the New Testament

It has become almost the orthodoxy of biblical scholarship to say that the world mission of the Church, as it began very early in Christian history, had nothing to do with the work of Jesus. Whatever might be found in the Gospels, the synoptics, or in John, which rings of this universalism, must be the early Church reading its mind back into the life of Jesus. I do not mean to deny that the concerns of the early Church have shaped the selection and editing of a great deal of what we now have in the canonical Gospels but we must listen to other testimony.

Considerable scholarship is now available on the proselytizing activities of the Jewish people before the conversion of Constantine to Christianity. Judaism at about the time of Christ and indeed aftertwards, was an actively proselytizing faith. It was the conversion of

Constantine, the official 'establishment' of the Christian Church and the emerging Byzantian imperial power which prevented Judaism from its proselytizing activities. We have echoes of this in the Gospels themselves: in Matthew 23 (the polemic against the Pharisees) Jesus says, 'for you traverse sea and land to make a single proselyte, and when he becomes a proselyte, you make him twice as much a child of hell as yourselves'.[5]

Could the ministry of Jesus then have been purely parochial when the Jews themselves were proselytizing? What liberation theologians call the Galilean crisis had turned the mind of Jesus to those who were on the fringes of Judaism at that time. His ministry in Galilee itself, Galilee of the Gentiles, a place that had been settled by the Assyrian conquerors with all sorts of people from Persia and further east, speaks not only of a commitment to the marginalized but to a plural context. The Galilean crisis turned Jesus' attention to those on the fringes in Galilee. The encounters with the centurion and the Syro-Phoenician woman give rise in Matthew to sayings like: 'Many will come from east and west and sit at table with Abraham, Isaac and Jacob.'[6]

The universalism of Matthew goes right back to the very beginning of the Gospel when the wise men come from the east, from the heart of the Zoroastrian cult itself. There is a case for saying that Jesus had a consciousness of the biblical universalism of the prophets. How could he not have had it? However, he may have changed his mind about how God's universal purpose was to be fulfilled, given the circumstances and frustrations in his public ministry.

—— Universalism of the Early Church ——

The early Church very quickly became universalist, not only in intention but in fact. One way of understanding the universalism of the early Church is to reflect on the traditions about the apostles. St Thomas went to India, Bartholomew probably to Persia, Andrew to Parthia and the Peloponnese, Peter to Antioch and then to Rome, and Paul, of course, throughout Asia Minor and Southern Europe and then to martyrdom in Rome. The apostles all have a universalist missionary history. From the very earliest times the gospel has had this universal appeal to every culture. The first nation to call itself Christian was Armenia. There was a Christendom, for better or for worse, in Ethiopia before there was one in Western Europe. The vigorous Christian churches of the Middle East were tamed only by the rise of Islam. There has been a Christian presence in the south of India from almost the very beginning of Christian history. The gospel made its appeal to every culture to which it was taken.

The Fathers continually speak of Christians as the third race, or as a new race. By that they mean that while Christians share some of the things of their particular culture, other things about them are so distinctive that they unite Christians from everywhere together over and against their parent culture. Throughout Christian history there has been a tension between inculturation on the one hand and universalism on the other. Because the gospel is universal it can make a particular appeal to a specific culture. It can take root in it and become so much part of it that it is difficult to imagine a culture without it. It forms a culture and its expression is formed by it. This one sees very clearly in people like the Armenians or the Assyrians, where to be Assyrian or Armenian is to be Christian. This has also been true of Ethiopians. I am deliberately giving examples from beyond Western Europe, because sometimes, as cultural anthropology has taught us, it is good to look at something beyond ourselves. In Western Europe too the gospel profoundly influenced the formation and emergence of culture, of nation states, and of systems, and was in turn affected by them. The problem is that as the gospel becomes contextualized into a particular culture, that in itself begins to constitute a barrier for other cultures; because Armenians are Christians, Azerbaijanis cannot be. And so Christians have always to be asking themselves what it is in the cult of Christianity, not the faith, which has to be put aside so that mission may be possible. Of course, the older a church, the longer the period for which a people have been Christian, the more urgent that question.

Theological Foundations of Universality – The Word

If the gospel is universal, what are the theological foundations of that universality? For Israel, it was simply a perception that the God who had liberated them from the power of Egypt must be a God who had such power over different peoples and nations. There are two ways, one broadly speaking Eastern and one broadly speaking Western, which theologically undergird this perception of the universality of the gospel. At the beginning of St John's Gospel in Chapter 1, sometimes called the Prologue to the Gospel, the evangelist speaks of the Eternal Word who is to become flesh. He claims that the same Word, who illuminates all human beings, is to come into the world in an 'embodied' or incarnate way. The Logos then illuminates all human beings who come into the world. There is, therefore, a presence of the Logos already in every culture. This is not to say that any culture is free of sin or to say that that sin does not obscure the presence of the Logos. The proclamation of the gospel, evangelism, is about the doing away of the obscuration of sin. But this seminal Word, Justin Martyr calls it the *Logos Spermatikos*, the scattered Word, is present in every human being, in every human culture. There is vigorous discussion in the Fathers about how the Eternal Word is present. Justin can claim that wherever there is truth or moral awareness, there people are Christian. The presence of the Word makes them Christian in some sort of way. Karl Rahner's understanding that there are 'anonymous Christians' outside the Church, has deep roots.[7] In Greek philosophy and in the classical poets, Justin and Clement of Alexandria were prepared to see the presence of the Logos. But they stop short, significantly, of seeing that presence in the popular religiosities around them. In fact, while Justin has very kind words to say about the philosophers and the poets, he has very hard words to say about the mystery religions.[8]

The Spirit

More common in the Eastern Fathers, and still used by Oriental and Eastern Orthodox in their approach to people of other faiths, is the presence of the Spirit in the world. If the Spirit, in fact, were not ahead of us in the world, there would be no Christians. Unless the Spirit can convict and convince people not only of their sin but of the possibility of salvation, we could not commit ourselves to the Lord in any way. In the farewell discourses in St John's Gospel, Jesus says that the Spirit is in the world, making the world aware, convincing the world, convicting the world, of righteousness, of sin and of judgement (John 16. 8–11). The *oikonomia* of the Spirit involves his presence and work in the world, witnessing to Christ and bringing people to faith in him.[9]

Anglican Tradition

The Anglican tradition speaks of Scripture, Tradition, and Reason as three ways in which human beings can think and speak abut the things of God. In a recent book, Bishop Lesslie Newbigin has attacked Anglicanism for this.[10] He points out that Rome has, in abandoning the two source theory regarding Scripture and Tradition, abandoned its dualism. For Vatican II speaks of Tradition as being the expositor of

Scripture. While Rome has abandoned its dualism, Anglicanism, Newbigin alleges, still sticks to its triad. He claims that there is no such thing as Christian Reason which is apart from Scripture and Tradition. In fact the Reason, he says, is embodied in the Tradition. Anglicanism is mistaken in seeing Reason as an autonomous source of authority.[11] Bishop Newbigin has perhaps misunderstood Anglicanism at this point. When Anglicans talk about Reason they do not mean that Reason is a source of authority. The sources of authority remain normatively Scripture and interpretatively Tradition. By Reason, Anglicans mean a human faculty which can evaluate and verify the claims made by Scripture and Christian Tradition.

The Caroline divines may have thought that Reason was a universal; that people in every culture, climate and country, had the same faculty of Reason and that if presented with the truths of Scripture or of Tradition this Reason would help them to accept these truths. But there is no such thing as a universal faculty of Reason which is the same in every culture and in every human society. Every society has its specific set of values, tradition, and intellectual idiom. But the gospel can make an appeal to the 'Reason' of every culture, and call it to account. What makes the gospel universal is not that reason is universal, but that the gospel can appeal to particular idioms, traditions, and sets of values, and can find responses among diverse peoples who hold to these diverse values, traditions, and intellectual idioms. And so when Anglicans now speak about Scripture, Tradition and Reason, I take it this is what they mean, and indeed official Anglican documents say this in so many words. The report of the Inter-Anglican Theological and Doctrinal Commission, *For the Sake of the Kingdom*, argues that the Anglican claim is that the truth of Scripture and of Christian Tradition is verified by every 'reason' in every culture. The weakness of Newbigin's 'conceptual fideism' is that it does not allow for adequate reflection on the interaction between the 'Reason' of the gospel tradition and the 'reason' of every culture, be it religious or secular.

—— Challenge to Cultic Christianity ——

Vincent Donovan, formerly a Roman Catholic missionary in Kenya, has written a book called *Christianity Rediscovered*.[12] The book is significantly sub-titled 'An Epistle *from* the Masai', the people in East Africa among whom he has worked. One of Donovan's concerns in this book is to begin to distinguish the traditional paraphernalia of Western missionary enterprise (compounds, schools and even clinics and hospitals), from the core of the gospel, which remains the offer of a new and transformed existence through faith in Jesus Christ, and its relation to human cultures. We have to say now that Christian mission must open up the Church to the most radical challenge about cultic Christianity. In fact if we do not challenge cultic Christianity, in whatever form, the whole Christian enterprise is endangered. Let me give you an example. The Christian Church is growing very rapidly in countries like Korea and Singapore, countries that are now known as NICs, newly industrialized countries. Technology has swept away the traditional values and religions of these countries. Christianity is stepping into and filling a vacuum. In other situations the Church is growing because colonialism has destroyed the traditional culture, including the religious culture, of people. Once again, Christianity is filling the vacuum. But the old values and systems that are disappearing in Western Europe are tied up with cultic Christianity. What is going to fill *that* vacuum?

When Dr Robert Runcie addressed concerns raised by the New Age movement, he was perhaps thinking along these lines. It is not that secularization has gone so far that religious concerns cannot any more be addressed, but that an old order, of which cultic Christianity is an integral part, has ceased to be credible for many people. A great danger in a venerable and established institution such as the Church of England is precisely that we may deceive ourselves. The great abbeys, cathedrals, the parochial system, and marvellous occasional services may lead us to think that all is well with this traditional cultic Christianity. But this is not so. The lesson of Christian mission today from Africa and Asia is that the old order is disappearing under the impact of technology and the intellectual challenges posed by technological development. If the gospel is not freed where it is implicated in the old order, then it will cease to make an impact.

—— *General Revelation* ——

Bishop Newbigin in the book that I have mentioned distinguishes between natural theology and revelation.[13] Natural theology, according to him, is an analogue of science. Just as I might endeavour to find out what a person is like by operating on his brain or his body and discovering his physiological and neurological systems, so a person might seek to discover the nature of God by observing the universe. I can get to know certain facts about a person by operating on him in this way but I will not get to know him as a person. As R. D. Laing, the well-known psychiatrist, put it, 'When we look into the brain, we do not see the sky, we see only brain.'[14] This is the way of natural theology. It has some value. We *do* arrive at *some* knowledge of God in this way but it is not a knowledge of personal encounter, which, Newbigin says, is reserved to 'revelation', which he regards as specific to the Judaeo-Christian tradition.[15]

——— *Salvation Histories* ———

This is a pretty bleak picture, if true. It leaves a whole mass of people, perhaps the majority, in the world today with only a 'natural' knowledge of God without the possibility of specific revelation to them. I would rather like to take the way of salvation history. There is not just a general revelation, natural theology, available to all people outside the Judaeo-Christian tradition. God has prepared each and every culture, each and every nation, each and every people in a specific way. 'Are you not like the Ethiopians to me, O people of Israel? Did I not bring up Israel from the land of Egypt, and the Philistines from Crete and the Syrians from Kir?' (Amos 9.7). Every nation, people and culture has a salvation history which must be specific to them. The question is, if this is so, how do we know what is salvation history among a particular people and what is sin, rebellion, and simply indifference? The biblical tradition is so valuable here because the salvation history, as recorded in the Bible, is normative for us in understanding the salvation histories of every people in this world. The salvation history in the Bible is not the *only* salvation history, but it *is* the normative one.

——— *The Decade of Evangelism* ———

The Anglican Church worldwide is in the midst of a decade of evangelism, and people have many questions about this decade. Why did the bishops, gathered together at the Lambeth Conference, call for a decade of evangelism? To answer this, we have to understand what constitutes evangelism, specially in the context of diverse cultures and religions. In the light of St John's first chapter, we have to understand evangelism as education, in the strict sense. Evangelism is 'a bringing out'. A few years ago in preparation for the San Antonio Conference on Mission, the World Council of Churches had a meeting to discuss evangelism. It was a vigorous meeting, because it represented a wide diversity of views. But in the end we came to an agreement about why evangelism was necessary. First, evangelism brings people to repentance, it causes people to turn around, to reorder their priorities. It is not only a turning *away* from sin but a turning *to* a new and transformed life. Second, evangelism brings about a fulfilment of all the authentic hopes and aspirations of human beings of every culture and faith. Third, and this is the educational point, it makes explicit what is implicit in human beings. It brings out what is there already. Fourth, it gives people, oppressed, poor and without hope, comfort and assurance.[16] The sharing of the gospel of a suffering God leads people to make sense of their own and the world's suffering. It leads to a high view of the significance of human life, not only created by God but redeemed by him. It leads to a confidence in human destiny, which is eternal fellowship with the loving and suffering God who has made this possible again at such great cost to himself.

We must reaffirm the truth that the preaching of the gospel brings about a crisis in human affairs which leads to conversion. At the same time, evangelization has to be recognized as a process in the formation of the People of God. Not only are the baptized evangelized by the preaching and the living of the gospel in the Church. Even the evangelists are evangelized by the gospel they preach (1 Cor. 9.23).

— 3 —

The Wholeness of Mission

✳

For the last century or so, Anglican theology has emphasized the centrality of the doctrine of the incarnation in our attempts to understand the nature of God.[1] What is true of the doctrine of God, however, must be true also of the doctrine of the Church, the Body of Christ. Those committed to belief in God incarnate must also be prepared to see the Church incarnated in the world. As a matter of fact, praxis has anticipated theology in this area. The origins and development of the parochial system show the strong commitment of Anglicanism to an incarnational way of understanding the relation of the Church to the world.[2] In fact such a commitment is discernible even in the period *before* the parochial system became firmly established. It is seen, for example, in the instructions given by Pope Gregory the Great to St Augustine of Canterbury. Augustine was charged not to destroy needlessly the culture of the pagan Anglo-Saxons. Even their shrines were not to be destroyed but were to be purified and consecrated for Christian use. Whatever could be preserved, without compromise, should be, and it should be pressed into the service of the gospel.[3]

—— The Question of Locality ——

The parochial system highlighted the presence of the Church in local communities. At the time of the Reformation, it was thought important to emphasize the relation of the Church to the *nation*. As I have said elsewhere, this had to do with an emerging consciousness of nationhood in sixteenth-century Europe.[4] For long, both local communities and the nation were relatively homogeneous and it was possible to relate the cultural and the communal, the geographical and the social to the Church in a somewhat simple way. In a multi-cultural, plural, society this becomes more and more difficult to do. It should not be imagined that Britain is now plural *only* in the sense that there

are significant ethnic minorities present here. An adequate understanding of contemporary British society must include a proper view of
the different subcultures which exist in the *indigenous* community as
well as the presence of ethnic minority cultures. The notion of a
subculture can enable us to discern community among people of a
particular band of professions, a specific style of life, interest in
particular forms of art or music, and even adherence to certain kinds of
spirituality. People today live according to a whole variety of world-
views, and this plurality of ideologies needs also to be taken seriously.
A question that needs to be posed in its sharpest form is whether the
Church continues to be incarnate in antiquated ways. Should the
principle of locality lead to the incarnation of the Church in the
different subcultures of contemporary Britain? There are indeed signs
that some at least are taking the subcultures seriously. The Restora-
tionist 'house-churches' are seeking to express their style of worship, if
not their organization, in terms that are easily accessible to popular
cultures. Church historians have commented on the consonance of the
emphasis on experience in some kinds of contemporary spirituality
with the high value given to experience in the modern world.[5] 'Cult'
congregations, even within mainline denominations, are seeking to
relate faith to life-style. In such an atmosphere, it is not enough to
reiterate the primacy of traditional structures, whether these are
parochial, diocesan, or national.

Of course, it is not only in Britain that the parochial system is under
pressure. In Latin America it is under pressure in a largely Roman
Catholic context. The shortage of clergy has often meant that the
parish priest is a remote figure and the parochial structures are seen as
distant. This sense of 'distance' has led small groups of Christians,
frequently in poor areas, to organize themselves into worshipping and
witnessing communities, largely independent of the parish priest and
the far away parish organization. The emergence of these ecclesial
communities is a new way of expressing incarnational presence in very
needy settings.[6]

In his address to the Lambeth Conference 1988, Bishop David Gitari
spoke of the need to adapt structures to pastoral and evangelistic need.
In his diocese they have discovered that parochial and even 'mission
station' structures are quite unsuitable for reaching the largely
nomadic peoples of Northern Kenya. They have had to develop ways
and means of ministry and mission which are themselves nomadic!
Pastors and evangelists now adopt the nomadic way of life of the
people they serve. This is the only way of being incarnational in such
contexts.[7]

In the highly urbanized societies of Japan, Korea, Singapore, and Hong Kong, on the other hand, the prohibitive price of land has often forced the Churches to rent apartments for use as places of worship. Necessity has, however, led to opportunity; a visible Christian presence is established in an apartment block, and this provides numerous occasions for witness and service. Fr Omaichi is a young Japanese priest working in the Northern diocese of Hokkaido. He has charge of a small 'apartment church' in the city of Sapporo. He lives, with his family, in another apartment next door to the church and is also the caretaker for the whole block! This latter role brings him into contact with every resident in the block and creates opportunities for sensitive witness.

In England, the parish church remains important as a focus for Christian presence and witness within a definite locality. The 'house-church' movement has, however, demonstrated that there are other ways of expressing such a presence and witness at the different levels of community life. Indeed, the emergence and proliferation of 'house-groups' within the mainline churches themselves has shown how it is possible, and even desirable, for Christians to come together in a whole number of non-traditional ways. On the whole, however, such 'house-groups' have had an orientation towards fellowship, worship, and Bible-study rather than witness and service. If, during the course of this decade, they could be inspired by the example of the basic communities to organize themselves for witness and service *in their immediate vicinity*, as well as to the wider community, this would be a signal advance. Under the leadership of Canon Peter Price, now General Secretary of the United Society for the Propagation of the Gospel (USPG), the insights gained from the basic communities *were* being brought to bear on parochial situations in the diocese of Southwark. This is an admirable illustration of how the world mission context impinges on local mission. It is to be hoped that this work will not only continue in the diocese but will spread to other parts of the country.[8]

—— *Incarnation and Identification* ——

The very nineteenth-century theologians who were emphasizing the centrality of the doctrine of the incarnation, of *skenosis* as it were, were also elaborating this doctrine in terms of *kenosis*, the self-emptying and self-limitation of the Eternal Word in taking human form (Phil. 2.7).[9] For an established Church, it is generally easier to understand incarnation in terms of presence rather than self-emptying. Even contemporary Church reports can say with pride that the parochial system 'still covers every inch of the country'. It is much more difficult to assess whether it is meeting the needs of every significant group within the population. In some situations, for example, is it catering for the needs of one segment of the population at the expense of others? Mere presence can be alienating if its visible form is palpably alien to significant sections of the population.

It is interesting, in this connection, to note that the Tractarian movement, which emphasized the belief that the Church was a divine institution over and against certain aspects of ecclesiastical establishment, also laid stress on the need for the Church to identify with the poor and needy. It is no accident, therefore, that well-known Anglican Catholic Churches and religious communities are to be found in areas that are, or once were, poor, and that the ministry of famous Catholic-minded clergy and religious was often among those on the margins of society. In this sense, there is a certain affinity between the Tractarians and evangelical movements such as the Salvation Army, the London City Mission and the Church Army.[10]

Evangelism and the Wholeness of Mission

Evangelism in such contexts in particular cannot be merely verbal, it must be an aspect of concern for the *whole* man and the *whole* woman. Certainly, Christian leaders in our partner Churches in Africa, Asia, and Latin America see mission in holistic terms. *They* would want to hold together proclamation and praxis, and they see declaration, dialogue, and *diakonia* as belonging together in the one mission of the Church. As Bishop Stephen Sykes has pointed out, evangelism is not so much a specific activity as an *attitude* informing a number of activities. The goal of *all* Christian witness and service will be to initiate people into the Kingdom of God.[11] Potentially, at any rate, all Christian witness and service bears an evangelistic value. Within the context of care for the whole person, there will be the concern for a person's spiritual destiny. This should lead to an open, but sensitive, sharing of faith and witnessing to God's work in Jesus Christ.

There is some evidence to suggest that *euangelizomai* and its Hebrew equivalent *bisser* do not only mean 'preaching' as the term has come to be understood. Rather, they mean a declaration of God's decision to right the wrongs suffered by the poor and oppressed. Such a declaration is based on a knowledge of God's saving acts in the *past* and it looks forward to a *future* free from oppression and injustice, but it is also about the *present*. It is not for nothing that Liberation theologians have referred to Luke 4.16–30 as 'The Nazareth Manifesto'. Here Jesus announces the programme for his own ministry; people are to be set free from their diseases, their hunger will be satisfied, their debts will be cancelled, and property from which they have been alienated will be returned. A year of jubilee will be proclaimed, and that is how the poor are evangelized (cf. Matt. 11.5).[12] Claus Westermann, commenting on the corresponding passage in Isaiah (61.1–4), has this to say: 'The dawning of the age of salvation proclaimed by the prophet, the great transformation, is also destined to work a change on the personal suffering of the large number of people who were actually suffering at the time.' He goes on to say that the prophet understands his ministry to be that of a herald announcing release, respite, and restoration.[13]

Evangelism and Words

It is clear, nevertheless, that whatever else evangelism may be, it is a calling, a declaring, a proclaiming. It is interesting to note, in this connection, that the typical New Testament word for such a proclamation, *kerusso*, is related to *kerygma*, the essential meaning of the gospel. In other words, we may say that the essential meaning of the gospel is disclosed in proclamation, though it is not, of course, exhausted by it. Christians need to live by the gospel and allow it to permeate every aspect of their lives, but the more they do this, the more necessary it becomes to explain to their friends, relatives, and colleagues *why* they behave in these ways – in the words of the New Testament they need to give 'an account of the hope that is in them' (1 Pet. 3.15).

It is well known that a great deal of the early Church's energy and time were spent in proclaiming the *kerygma*. If we examine the speeches in the Acts of the Apostles, we find that the central truths of God's presence and work in the life, passion, and resurrection of Jesus Christ from the dead are repeated again and again. At the same time, we also find that this proclamation is related to the immediate situation and beliefs of each audience. If the audience is predominantly Jewish, the proclamation of the *kerygma* is placed within the context of salvation history as it was understood by the Jewish people of the time (e.g., Acts 2.14–47; 3.11–26; 7.1–53; 13.16–41). If, on the other hand, the audience is mainly Gentile, an attempt is made to begin with whatever is authentic in *their* tradition. This is then related to God's revelation in Christ (Acts 10.34–43; 14.8–18; 17.22–34).[14] This practice of contextualizing the *kerygma* is continued in the early Fathers of the Church. Justin Martyr, for example, relates the coming of Christ to the teachings of the prophets in his conversations with the Jews. In his apology to the Roman Emperor, on the other hand, he speaks of Jesus Christ as being the embodiment of the Logos, or universal reason, who inspires love of truth, goodness, and beauty in all human beings.[15]

In every epoch of the Church's mission, the gospel has had to be embodied in the vocabulary, thought-forms and traditions of various peoples. The expression and mediation of the gospel in terms of a particular culture requires extended dialogue with the people of that culture. Such a dialogue has to include discussion of a people's intellectual, moral, and aesthetic tradition but, most of all, it needs to be about their spiritual tradition, or the ways in which they make sense of the world and the meaning they give to their own life. Without a deep understanding of a people's world-view, evangelists or missionaries will not be able to communicate the gospel to the people among whom they are placed. There is no question of 'targeting' communities, and especially the vulnerable among them, but there *is* a need to present the gospel in ways that are intelligible to people with a particular background and tradition.

Some missiologists distinguish between the *inculturation* of the gospel, by which they mean its expression in terms of a people's tradition and background, and its *contextualization*. By this latter term, they mean the ways in which the gospel addresses a people's social, economic, and political situation, particularly in terms of justice for the poor and liberation for the oppressed. Both the process of inculturation and that of contextualization have very far reaching effects on the lives of the people concerned. They influence not only the ways in which people think and worship but also social customs such as rites of passage, institutions such as caste and class, and fundamental human values such as attitudes to money, possessions, and power. Both processes need to continue in Christian communities as they change and develop. The *kerygma* itself, that is the proclamation of God's saving work in Christ, is one limitation on the two processes. Nothing should be done which compromises the integrity of the gospel. The other limitation is the necessity of fellowship between the churches. Anything which hinders such fellowship should be avoided.[16] Another way of putting this is to say that authentic inculturation is discerned by means of *criteria* which include fidelity to Scripture and the maintenance and enhancement of the world-wide Church's unity in faith.

Evangelism and Witness

If *kerygma* has to do with proclaiming God's saving acts, *marturia* has to do with bearing costly witness as to how God's work in Christ has affected our lives. The most costly way to do this is, of course, to die for the Faith. Numerous Christians right down the ages have done just this; they have accepted death rather than renounce or hide their faith. Such a courageous testimony to hope based on faith has often had the result of vindicating the Faith itself. One of Athanasius' central arguments for the truth of Christ's resurrection was based on the observed reality that Christians of all kinds, men, women, children, the old and the young, were willing to die for their belief that God had raised Jesus Christ from the dead, and would raise them to a transformed life in a similar manner.[17] It is a matter of shame that such an argument cannot be used in so many parts of the contemporary Church, though this century too, as the Archbishop of Canterbury has pointed out, can be called a century of martyrs.

Marturia is not just about martyrdom, of course. It is about bearing costly witness. It appears that immediately after the apostolic age, there were comparatively few 'full-time' evangelists and missionaries. The Faith spread mainly through the verbal and lived testimonies of Christians in homes, at the workplace and even in court! The forbearance of a Christian wife living with a pagan husband, the fidelity of a daughter to the Christian Faith in the face of parental pressure and a determination not to yield to the blandishments of imperial officers, all of these are well-attested examples of *marturia*.[18]

In our own times too, there have been many Christians who have borne a costly witness to the gospel. They may have done this simply by believing that God has revealed himself in Jesus Christ, and suffering because of this belief. It is also possible that they have stood for particular gospel values, such as the equal dignity of all human beings created in God's image or the need for justice and compassion in society. They may have opposed tyrants who had taken away their people's basic rights, or institutions which discriminated against people because of their race or gender. In some countries, Christian leaders are the only ones who can oppose tyranny and oppression. The role of bishops in both Eastern and Southern Africa in recent times is a remarkable example of how Christian leaders can bear witness to fundamental gospel values in the face of oppression. Such a leadership has been exercised in response to the demands of Christian discipleship, but it has certainly had the effect of making the gospel credible – and not only in Eastern and Southern Africa!

Christian witness in difficult social and political contexts is not aimed at the overthrow of the existing order so that it can be replaced by a 'Christian' one. It is aimed rather at 'modelling' an order that conforms more closely to the demands of the Kingdom of God. It is obvious that such modelling must first take place in Christian communities themselves and then in wider communities where Christians have influence. Within institutions and communities Christians will want to subvert false values based on selfishness, greed, and cruelty, and will seek to transform institutions and communities by promoting gospel values within them. Where Christians do not have enough influence within institutions and communities, they may seek to bring about change through campaigning and public education. The emergence, in recent years, of Christian-led coalitions against apartheid, child exploitation, homelessness and other social and political issues is an example of how effective such campaigning can be. The aim, once again, is not so much to overthrow a system but to transform it so that its evil aspects are challenged and changed, and the good is promoted. As Bishop Lesslie Newbigin has said, the victory of the Church over the Roman Empire was not won by seizing the levers of power; it was won when the victims knelt down in the Colosseum and prayed in the name of Jesus for the Emperor![19] It is true that, in extremis, there may be systems that are so blatantly and incorrigibly evil that only their overthrow can be the beginning of something new. In such cases Christians may, with reluctance, give support to the overthrow of such systems – but only as a last resort and without ambition for power. When a new order is in place, they will seek to work within it as salt and light – through example and persuasion, never by diktat.

—— Evangelism and Worship ——

Leitourgia or worship is, first of all, offering praise, thanksgiving and adoration to God, but it is also a powerful means of witness to the world. The New Testament clearly recognizes the significance of worship for witness. This is seen not only in thanksgiving and adoration but in the fellowship among Christians and in the just and equal treatment of all, believers as well as those who are not yet believers (Acts 2.43–47; 1 Cor. 14.23–25; Jas 2.1–7). It is true that in the sub-apostolic period, because of the fear of persecution, worship was increasingly restricted to Christians only. Even so, the early apologists often refer to Christian worship, either to defend it against pagan attacks or, more positively, to show how truth and love are promoted by the worship of Christians.[20]

It is interesting to note that churches which have a well-developed view of worship as witness are often those which have been restricted in other forms of witness. The ancient oriental churches in the heartlands of Islam, for example, although they had effective missionary work outside their own contexts, were denied opportunites for evangelism at home. This led them to develop a view of the liturgy itself as an occasion for witness. Nor was this confined to the rite: church architecture, posture, iconography and the devotion of the congregation were all understood as aspects of witness.[21] In more recent years, churches in Marxist countries have experienced similar restrictions. Once again, they have concentrated on making their worship an effective means of witness.

One of the striking features of Christianity in many parts of Africa, Asia, and Latin America has to do with the *visibility* of worship in public places such as parks. Parading to and from church also makes worship more visible to the world. In colder climates and more privatized cultures, such visibility is more difficult to achieve. Processions have traditionally been one of the ways in which worship is made visible, and there is something of a revival going on these days as far as they are concerned. The media too are providing newer opportunities for making worship visible. It is important that such visibility should be maintained and enhanced while new structures are being put in place. Parishes and dioceses are organizing more out-of-doors worship. Such a trend needs to be encouraged and assisted to become more effective. In the end, however, it is the question of church buildings themselves which needs to be addressed. In an interesting experiment, a church on a housing estate has used plate glass for the whole of its west wall. This makes worship and other activities of the congregation 'transparent' to the whole community. Newer church buildings are often 'multi-purpose', and if the part set aside for worship is carefully integrated with the rest of the building, this can give people 'access' to Christian worship in an undemanding and non-pressurized way.

Historic buildings cannot be easily altered but they often attract visitors, and an effective ministry to visitors could be a significant way of outreach for parishes with historic buildings. Parochial Church Councils (PCCs) and congregations need to respond to this challenge in terms of funds and time which are made available for this ministry. Cathedrals, on the whole, are well-organized to deal with large numbers of visitors but in some cases, at least, there needs to be more self-conscious effort to make worship accessible and attractive to visitors. It is perhaps worth saying that cathedrals in France, where the Church does not have to maintain the fabric of the buildings, have excellent systems of pastoral care for the visitors. Worship is more visible and more accessible, and there seems to be a greater availability of clergy and religious.

One of the achievements of the Anglican Reformation lay in the emergence of a liturgical tradition which managed to combine a sense of mystery in worship with *accessibility* to it for ordinary people. The medieval rites certainly conveyed a sense of mystery, but were inaccessible in terms of language and participation. Cranmer's greatest achievement, the rendering of the liturgy in a tongue 'understanded of the people', is also a charter for contemporary Anglicanism in taking the task of inculturation in worship seriously. In nearly every part of the Anglican Communion there is a great desire to relate worship to the surrounding culture. Many new rites have been produced and some others are being prepared for use. Perhaps the most useful thing that liturgists can do is to provide the churches with flexible rites and other material which can easily be adapted for specific situations. One can no longer assume that national cultures will be homogeneous. The rites need to provide a uniformity in the basic pattern, while allowing for variety as the churches seek to address the local cultures and sub-cultures around them.

Worship has also to do with the *availability* of Christians for witness. As Bishop Stephen Sykes has said, contrition and praise bring about a peace and joy which the world cannot give. These impel Christians to share their faith with others. Those who praise God in the congregation are led to praise him in the world.[22]

—— Evangelism and Works of Love ——

In his attitude to the poor, Jesus stood four-square within the prophetic tradition of the Old Testament. Like John the Baptist before him, he was passionately committed to justice for the poor but he also had compassion on them and love for them. These were demonstrated in his ministry of healing, feeding, and teaching among them. This concern for and love of the poor and all those in any kind of need continues to be demonstrated throughout the New Testament (Acts 2.45; 3.1–10; 6.1–6; 11.27–30; Rom. 12.3–21, 2 Cor. 8 and 9, Jas. 1.27—2.17). In the period after that of the apostles, the early Christians too continued to visit poor parts of the cities; feeding the poor, treating their diseases, and burying the dead. They gave generously to orphans, slaves, and those in prison. Their love of the poor had to do with their love for the Lord himself who, 'though he was rich, yet for our sakes became poor' (2 Cor. 8.9). It had also to do with the evangelical counsel of poverty which demanded that Christians should be prepared to give up their all for the sake of the Kingdom of God (Mark 10.17–31 and parallels). In other words, their love of the poor was formed by their memory of how Jesus himself had lived and their understanding of the life-style to which he called them.[23]

Throughout history, Christians have been active in helping the poor and disadvantaged. Both universal education and medical treatment for all may be traced back to Christian initiatives. Christians have been heavily involved in the campaign for the abolition of slavery, in improvements in the conditions of life for working men and women, and in the struggle for equal rights for women.[24] It is true that from time to time Christians and Churches have not been faithful to the gospel and have compromised with those who have oppressed the poor. The gospel itself, however, has been a witness against them and, in many cases, faithful Christians have borne a costly witness to the authentic teaching of the gospel.

A significant feature of our own times is the large number of the poor who have been formed by the gospel and who are witnessing to the gospel's demand for justice. They have an important ministry in the universal church.[25]

Those engaged in authentic *diakonia*, or Christian service, do it, of course, for the sake of their Lord and because of their love for the poor.[26] Such service, nevertheless, has great value as witness and does much for the credibility of the gospel. It is not only that such service disposes individuals and communities to a favourable hearing of the gospel. Nor is it only that evangelism and social action must always go together. It is rather that *diakonia* itself has an evangelizing dimension. Mother Teresa of Calcutta and her Sisters of Charity, for example, are not evangelists in the usual sense of the term, but their work has been shown to have important evangelistic significance, not only among the poor but for the many around the world who take an interest in it. Because of their work, people like Malcolm Muggeridge have been moved to consider seriously the Faith which results in such fruit.

——— *Uniqueness and Universality* ———

A properly universal view of God is necessary for an adequate understanding of world mission today. God *does* reveal himself in the particular and the specific, but this is so that his activity everywhere and in all may properly be discerned. Special revelation can be the norm or yardstick by which God's presence and work elsewhere is to be judged and discerned. This is specially so of God's revelation in Christ; this enables us to discern how God has worked in the history of Israel as well as in those of other nations, peoples, and cultures.

While it is biblical, and in accordance with primitive tradition, to believe that God is preparing each people, and indeed each individual, for his salvation, this need not necessarily be through the dominant religious tradition of a people. In Asia, at least, people are becoming more and more aware that dominant religious traditions (including Christian manifestations of them) have often served the cause of oppressors. The 'salvation-history' of a people then may be seen in how they have resisted oppression, in their turning of suffering to good effect, in alternative spiritualities perhaps, and in their celebration of life in poetry, drama, and music.[27] People may be prepared for salvation by signs of the Logos' ordering presence in the world around them, in the rationality of their own minds, and in the ordered structures of society (insofar as they are just and life-enhancing). They may also be prepared by the work of the Holy Spirit in their lives, bringing them to a sense of themselves and of God. Sin, however, is also a reality and obscures much of the Logos' presence and the work of the Spirit. If the 'potential' for salvation is to become 'actual' in every person and every people, it is necessary that people should come to a consciousness of their rebellion against God, their abuse of the world and of themselves, and that, realizing their weakness, they should throw themselves on God's mercy. Sir Norman Anderson has often suggested that this can happen in the context of other religious traditions. Such people, he claims, are not saved by the practice of their religion or by 'good works' but because they have sought God's mercy.[28] Even such a situation is perilous, however, for how can people *know* that God has answered their cry?

We have the paradox then of the Logos, the informing reason of the universe, disposing people and cultures towards fulfilment in him and, at the same time, sin, in both its social and personal aspects, obscuring and negating the work of the Logos and his Spirit. Is there a way out of such an impasse? It is here that the idea of special revelation can be helpful. Such a revelation will cohere with what people already know of goodness and of God, though it will also challenge whatever is false about human beings and their beliefs. It will have the capacity to free people from their slavery to sin and to set them on the path of true freedom. For Christians, the revelation in Jesus Christ is, *par excellence*, such a revelation. He sums up all revelation in himself, and it is by reference to him that Christians recognize the authenticity of any revelation. It is true, of course, that such claims about the uniqueness of Christ cannot be settled a priori. They depend, rather, on our estimate of his person and work. It is for this reason that liberation theologians, while acknowledging the necessity for biblical criticism, have insisted on the recoverability of the 'historical Jesus'.[29] Are the graciousness and originality of his teaching such that we can see him as the unique revelation of God's Word? Do his healing, feeding, and discipling reveal God's power in a way not seen elsewhere? Do his suffering and death reveal a God profoundly involved in the bringing to perfection of a manifestly imperfect universe? Does his resurrection show uniquely how God can transform suffering, endured for his sake, into something glorious? Does encounter with Jesus Christ, as he is portrayed in the New Testament and preached in the Church, bring people to a consciousness of their own inadequacy before God? There is an implicit recognition of the Logos in all human beings; does Jesus Christ reveal him in such a way that the implicit becomes explicit, so that in following him we are able to fulfil God's purposes for us? To those who have come to know their own sin and their need of God, does Jesus Christ bring assurance of the forgiveness of sins?

It is in answers to questions such as these that worthy motives for contemporary evangelism will be found. Christians need to take the reality of sin very seriously, but, to engage in authentic evangelism, they do not need to deny whatever is true, good, and beautiful in human thought, art, technology, structures of society and even spirituality. They need, rather, to affirm that such truth, goodness, and beauty are from the eternal Logos, who is uniquely revealed in Jesus Christ, and find their fulfilment in him.

> Of the Father's heart begotten,
> Ere the world from chaos rose,
> He is Alpha: from that Fountain
> All that is and hath been flows,
> He is Omega, of all things
> Yet to come the mystic close,
> Evermore and Evermore.[30]

— 4 —
Thinking Theologically About Development

*

In seeking to provide a theological underpinning for a commitment to development, I must begin with our doctrine of *God*, so when we consider theology we are actually beginning with the proper subject for theology, that is, God.

If you imagine God to be perfect and complete in himself, if you imagine him to be beyond change, a question might arise: why should such a God create a world at all? And, indeed, this was a question that the Fathers of the Church were facing continually. But if you thought that he *would* create a world, then the world that such a God would create would be a perfect world, a world that was complete in every respect. Any corruption, any imperfection in that world would, of necessity, have to be brought about by creatures, not by the Creator.

But think again of God who is perfect in his faithfulness, who is unchangeable in his purpose, in the steadfastness of his purpose, but who is also capable of change, capable of suffering, for example. What sort of world would such a God create? I think we can say that he would create freely and spontaneously. He would create a world that was not complete yet, but he would be working to bring such a world to perfection.

And, of course, such a God would be affected by the imperfection and the suffering of this world. Now I find that the biblical evidence is much more in favour of belief in a picture of God, in language about God, in the latter sense.

— A Tremendous Task —

God has, of course, created human beings as stewards and as fellow workers with him in this task of perfecting creation. Bill Vanstone, in that wonderful book *Love's Endeavour, Love's Expense*, points out that, in creating at all, God has taken a tremendous risk because by creating another, something other than himself, he has created something that is not wholly plastic to his purposes, something that has resistance in itself because it is other than God. In such a creation, things can and do go wrong but God, Bill Vanstone writes, has not abandoned the world; he continues to work redemptively in it.[1]

The Marred Image

What can be said of physical creation can equally be said, perhaps more so, of human beings, of human societies, of people with freedom and the power to exercise choice. Wrong choices can be made and, indeed, are made. Human beings, by choosing wrongly, have corrupted not only the physical world but also their own communities, their own societies and, indeed, themselves.

Once again, God has not abandoned human society. The image of God in human beings may be marred but it has not been destroyed, and God continues to work redemptively in human societies, among human beings.

The Disclosure of His Will

Now we know this is so because we know of God's mighty acts in history. We know of the disclosure of his will in the message of the prophets and, of course, we know of his great disclosure in the living and the dying and the rising again of Jesus Christ from the dead.

In Christ, we find the God who suffers and who loves and who is patient with his creation. We find a God who has not abandoned even a deeply marred creation but who seeks to redeem it and to transform it. And in Christ we see that this commitment to the creation is to the point of incarnation, it is not simply working at a distance.

The Church in the World

From one point of view, the Church is a company of fallible, but forgiven sinners; that is true. But from another point of view, the Church is the body of Christ, and continues God's commitment in incarnation, shown in the living and the dying and the rising again of Jesus Christ.

The Church, then, is placed in the world and is placed among human societies and has to come to an estimate of these societies. The gospel that the Church brings to the world can never become intelligible until the Church has tried to affirm whatever remains true and good and beautiful in human society.[2] The gospel can only be mediated when the Church and a particular society are speaking the same language, and it ceases to be mediated when, on either side, we stop speaking the same language.

So the need for community between Church and world is very great. Every society has its informing principles, its values, its beliefs, its world-view, and it is right that the Church, in the proclamation of the gospel, should affirm whatever it can of these values, beliefs and world-views.

—— Principalities and Powers ——

There are, however, things that have gone wrong with people's values, with world-views, with beliefs, and so the Church is also called, in the light of the gospel, to judge what has gone wrong.

Bishop Lesslie Newbigin has pointed out that every society, every community, needs what he calls 'principalities and powers', informing principles that actually allow a society or a community to work. These principles may inform the spirit of a school, or of patriotism, or they may contribute to a pride in your town. There is nothing wrong with these things but, of course, we all know that they can go horribly wrong. Patriotism can become fanatical racist nationalism, for instance. We are seeing some of that happening once again in parts of Europe.

So the Church needs, then, to be able, in the light of the gospel, to point out where the 'principalities and powers' have become independent of God and, indeed, have rebelled against God.[3]

—— Salvation History ——

The Church can do this because it knows of God's will as it has been disclosed in his mighty acts and through the prophets, and in the incarnation of our Lord Jesus Christ, our Saviour. Salvation history provides the necessary criterion for the Church to relate to society both affirmatively and negatively. In other words, in every community, in every society, in every culture, the Church can look for what is life-affirming, what is positive, what is for the building up of a community, because of how God has acted in history and how that has been received in the Church's tradition.

At the same time, the Church can tell what is life-denying, what destroys community because, once again, of the witness that we find in the history of God's people.

—— *Concern for the Poor* ——

From its earliest days the Church has had a concern for the poor, for those less fortunate. We can see in the early history of the Church, for example, a great desire among the early Christians to free slaves – that was a good work that a Christian, if he or she had enough wealth, was called to do, even at the time when slavery as an institution was not being challenged; to visit those in prison; to go to the most disreputable parts of a city.

One of the things to which Roman husbands with Christian wives objected was that their Christian faith led such wives to visit the most disreputable parts of a city.

—— *The Way of Poverty* ——

W. H. C. Frend has pointed out that the Christian Church was socially the most mobile of communities in the ancient world, that people could expect to find social equality within the Church if not outside it.[4] The Church's work among the poor was not unique, of course. There were many well-placed and well-disposed pagans who also worked among the poor and were generous to those less fortunate than themselves. But Gregory of Nazianzus, for example, points out that the difference between Christians' commitment to the poor and pagan generosity was that the Christians *loved* the poor. He gives different reasons for this, one of them being that 'our Lord Jesus Christ himself though he was rich yet for our sakes became poor' (2 Cor. 8.9). Another was Jesus' challenge to us to follow in the way of poverty, what has come to be known as the evangelical counsel of poverty.[5]

—— *Christian Commitment* ——

As we have seen already, this commitment to the poor, *mutatis mutandis*, in one way or another, has continued in the history of the Church, even though there have been many in the Church who have actually oppressed the poor. The commitment has continued, for example, in the provision of medical care or of universal education in which we find that Christian churches have played a major role.

Even in the eighteenth and nineteenth centuries the campaign for the abolition of the slave trade, and later of slavery itself, was something in which Christians were prominent. The campaigns to provide better working conditions and just wages for working men, women and children in this country, were, once again, areas where committed Christian people were prominent.[6] Elaine Storkey has pointed out how Christian women were prominent, in the nineteenth century, in working for the enfranchisement of women and for full rights for them in different fields.[7]

This commitment, as I say, has continued through history and in different cultures and on different continents.

—— *The Pragmatic Epoch* ——

Charles Elliot divides this kind of commitment to the poor into three categories, or three epochs.[8]

First, he writes, there was the *pragmatic* period when the Church tried to help the poor by raising their living standards, by providing better medical care for them, by providing education for them, and by ensuring that they had enough to eat. He calls this the pragmatic, or the missionary, approach.

Now, I think he has been, if I may say so, a little unkind because, even in the early period of the modern missionary movement, while it is true that many missionaries were concerned simply to better the living conditions of people in this way and, perhaps, were unconsciously playing into the hands of colonial policy, on other occasions we find that Christian people involved in mission actually challenged colonial policy. For example, this proved to be the case in the matter of slavery in the Caribbean.

We find too that, already in the eighteenth century, Christians were providing a robust challenge to attitudes to caste in India, campaigning for the rights of women there, particularly married women. They mounted a serious challenge, too, to the way in which mineworkers were treated in Central Africa later in the nineteenth century.

These were not just matters of pragmatism, of providing better medicine or education for people. These challenges arose out of a deep commitment to the gospel and an awareness of how God acts in a liberating way.

—— *The Developmental Period* ——

The second period that Elliot identifies is what he calls the *developmental* one. This was a period after the Second World War, when many churches, particularly in the Western world, began to develop church-related agencies, partly in order to carry out the work of reconstruction in Europe that needed to be done. Elliot points out that many international and denominational and inter-denominational agencies owe their origins to this time. Christian Aid, for instance, are beginning to think about celebrating the fiftieth anniversary of their work, which has its roots in inter-church aid initiated for the reconstruction of post-war Europe.

Elliot's criticism of this phase is that it was not properly theologically based, that its theological underpinning was somewhat weak and relied on rather hazy notions such as 'global neighbourhood'.

Nevertheless, once again I am bound to say that if these agencies had not been established in the post-war period, our ability to respond to the massive problems of refugees, of famine, and of civil conflict in the world today, would have been severely reduced. It is because these agencies exist that we can respond reasonably quickly to such situations. And so, perhaps, developmentalism, as a phase, needed to exist.

—— The Structural Phase ——

The third phase that Elliot identifies is what he calls the *structural* approach to development and he relates this to the rediscovery by Christians of the centrality of justice and mercy in the Bible. People began to see how central these concerns were, not only to the prophets in the Old Testament but to the teaching of Jesus himself and to the practice of the early Church.

The structural approach, then, is about justice. It is about struggle against those structures in the world, or indeed in the Church, which are oppressive, which are unjust to one group of people or another and, of course, there are dramatic examples of such structural injustice and the struggle against it. The resistance of Christian churches to apartheid in South Africa is one example, but the struggle by different women's groups in many different parts of the world for an end to discrimination on grounds of gender is another. The struggle by outcaste people, the *dalits*, in India against being defined through birth as the most despised group in that society, is yet another.

—— Addressing All Three Strands ——

Now the thing about Elliot's three periods is that in any Church, or even in any development agency, all of these co-exist, as far as I can see. It seems evident that every Church and every development agency has to respond pragmatically to human need as and when it occurs. We can do no other; sometimes we just have to meet the immediate need.

Neither has the developmental approach ended. More and more charities devoted to the cause of development are coming into being all the time. And, of course, the structural response continues to be relevant because there are still many areas of injustice in society that need to be addressed.

—— Significant Human Identity ——

How, then, are we to think of a programme for the world-wide Church of God today in addressing development?

The Church needs first to affirm once again the significance of *human identity* – that human beings have an inherent worth, dignity, and value which have been given to them because they have been created in God's image. I am delighted that so much of post-modern culture actually takes the inherent dignity of human beings for granted and I think that this must be one of the connections that the Church has with post-modern culture today. Some of this we may, in fact, owe to that much abused phenomenon of the Enlightenment. The Church must affirm the inherent worth of human beings. A Korean priest was asked recently about the Decade of Evangelism and he said that to make a human person aware of his or her worth is a kind of evangelism.

But this identity is not lived out in isolation. It is profoundly an identity in community. All of us find out who we are, what we are called to do, what we are called to become, by being in community – in natural communities of family, or village, or tribe, or whatever it may be, or, indeed, in the community of Christ, in the Church.

—— Transformation and Renewal ——

The importance of human identity leads me to point out the significance of *transformation* and *renewal* in development. These are words, *metamorphosis* and *anakainosis*, that are used again and again in the New Testament. As Christians we should be able to affirm gladly that human development, the development of human communities, hinges profoundly on inner transformation and renewal, that without these changes we are only into manipulating people and other resources.

Of course, this transformation and this renewal need to come about first of all in the oppressors, for instance, those who are not paying a fair wage for a fair day's work, those who are not paying a just price for

43

a product which they are buying. The notions of a just wage and of a fair price are not modern notions, they are deeply rooted in medieval Christian ethics.

Transformation has to come about first, then, in the powerful, the oppressors, those who have the advantage in life. But it also needs to come about in those who are oppressed, those who have been wronged, those who have had advantage taken of them, because it is a truism to say that the oppressed, if they become oppressors, can be the worst kind of oppressors. The oppressed know how to oppress those even less fortunate than themselves.

Development is not 'all in the mind', don't ever believe that, but it *is* *also* in the mind. We need a shift in attitude, we need conversion, we need a new perspective if development is to work. This has to be so both in communities that are powerful and in communities that are powerless; and 'powerful' and 'powerless' are relative terms, there is a whole gradation of communities from the very powerful to the utterly powerless.

—— *Paradigm Events* ——

Let me give you an example of what such transformation might be like. In the diocese of which I was bishop, there was a group of people who were professional beggars. For five thousand years they have been members of a caste whose job has been to beg. Everybody expects them to beg, they themselves expect to beg and they do nothing else.

A very small group of Christians began to work among them in different ways and one of the main things that they wanted to achieve in this group of beggars was literacy, to pass on to at least some of them the ability to read and to write. After some months, one girl volunteered to follow this programme of study. Her fellow beggars were so sceptical that this could happen in their community. None of them had ever read or written before, why should they suddenly be able to read or write now? After some time, this girl was able to stand up in the community and to read a simple passage from the Bible. Now that changed the community's perspective, that was a kind of 'paradigm event': they suddenly realized that they could read and write as well as anyone else!

That kind of transformation is needed. In another part of the world, a doctor, who wanted to bring some kind of sanitation to a village, found that only children would co-operate with him. So he started teaching the children because the adults wouldn't listen and, gradually, as he did things with the children, the grown-ups got interested. They started watching and, later, participating until, finally, there was a sanitation programme in the whole of that region, not only in that village! So transformation and renewal are basic to development.

—— *Care* ——

Some other categories important to development I have titled *care, conscientization* and *campaigning*.

There are some communities in the world where involvement in development has to begin with remaking broken communities and broken human beings. These people are not able to engage in what we might think are developmental projects because they have been so broken by suffering. The many refugees in different parts of the world are examples of this.

Now unless these people are allowed to re-group, to establish community, to build basic shelters for themselves, development among them cannot begin, and care is a necessary prelude to it. Of course, as soon as they have got shelter and some kind of assurance of food supplies, they then begin to ask other very interesting questions. In one case, recently displaced people from the Sudan began to ask about education for their children. Their greatest need they felt, once their food supply had been assured, was paper or slates because children were being taught to write in the sand!

—— *Conscientization* ——

Second, there is conscientization. Once again, like transformation and renewal, conscientization is something that takes place at, at least, two ends of a 'relationship'. There is the conscientization of those who are causing injustice, of those who are causing oppression, even unwittingly, bringing them to an awareness of what it is that they are a part. One of the great achievements of liberation theology has been that it has made the Church in Latin America, especially the Roman Catholic Church, deeply aware of its participation in the oppression of its own people. However, conscientization also needs to take place at the other end of the link, among the oppressed.

If you ask me what the difference is between transformation, on the one hand, and conscientization, on the other, I might say transformation has to do with a whole new perspective on life, whereas conscientization, very often, is about something particular or some particular matters, some particular elements in life.

Let me give you an example. In the 1960s and 1970s, the Christian churches in south-west Asia discovered that those making bricks in traditional brick-kiln factories were perhaps the most oppressed people in that area. The technology was traditional, hardly changed since the days of the Exodus. They were paid on the piece-work principle, so that if it rained or whatever, they wouldn't get paid at all! They were usually in huge debt to their employer, so they could not actually change their employment; they could not improve themselves; the facilities that were provided for them at their place of work were minimal; there was no schooling for children; no medical help, nothing like that at all. One of the worst evils was that these people did not know that any other kind of life was even possible.

Now, the churches and their agencies went in and they were allowed to do so, of course, because some of these people were Christians and all the employers would allow was the practice of religion – on the principle that religion might be an opiate that would keep them unaware of their condition.

But through this very traditional inroad into a very oppressive system, change began to come to these communities. They began to see that a different life might be possible – if not for them, then at least for their children.

Gradually, the churches were able to interest human rights organizations, and even the courts, in the plight of these people, and so, now, we have a situation where real change may yet be possible through legislation, through awareness of the oppressed themselves and the churches' own programmes for development.

—— Campaigning ——

Campaigning has inevitably a political aspect to it. Recent provisions of charity law tend to assume that charitable work which aims at changing the condition of the poor can be done apolitically. This is difficult to believe. When you are acting in the interests of the poor and, therefore, *against* vested interests, there is inevitably a political aspect to it.

It should not become 'party political' if that can be helped, though there will be allies in different political parties for one kind of action or another. But to say that charitable work must remain apolitical is really to render it ineffective in terms of bringing about structural change in the world.

—— *Participation and Empowerment* ——

All development must be such that the poor are able to *participate* in the definition of what it is that they want, in seeking to achieve it, in working to achieve it, and the result of such development must be their empowerment. It is not always so but that is how it should be.

One of the most worrying aspects of the condition of the poor is the widespread alienation of the poor from the land, from factors of production, from opportunities for education. Empowering the poor for stewardship has to be about ending that alienation.

One of the strongest criticisms that I have of the work of the IMF and the World Bank in many different parts of the world is that it has relied so heavily on the 'trickle down' effect. So it has emphasized working with the relatively rich in the hope that, by making the comparatively rich richer, the poor will somehow be helped, but this has not happened in most parts of the world that I know.

And so there is a need today to re-define official and voluntary development policy in such a way that there is an emphasis on the poorest of the poor. This is why I think Christian Aid's basic mission commitment to strengthen the poor is so important and we need to identify non-governmental voluntary agencies among the poor to be our partners in this. It is good to note that international agencies are at last taking local NGOs seriously.

Land reform; the rights of minorities, particularly aboriginal minorities, to ancient lands; the encouragement of the poor in what has come to be called micro-enterprise, in which the poor are encouraged to begin some kind of business activity that not only provides an income for them but provides, perhaps, employment for some others – these are some of the ways in which the alienation of the poor from the land and from factors of production can be challenged.

—— *Co-creators with God* ——

There has been, among Christians concerned for development, a fundamental tension between *education* and *action*.

If you look at the several World Council of Churches-sponsored conferences on Church and Society, the emphasis has been particularly on forming the Christian mind so that Christians could then, in their own context, act for justice. But in the 1960s and 1970s it was discovered that this was not enough because it only addressed a certain kind of person who could participate in this kind of formation, so some people began to talk of taking the line of direct action. Such a view considers social struggle necessary for the securing of justice in society.

To participate in such a struggle, churches and Christians need to find *community* with the poor, they need to take their side in the *conflict* which is inevitable if justice is to be secured. They need to promote *conscientization* among the poor of their rights and they need to be committed to the liberation of the poor so they can be *co-creators* with God of their own future.

In the World Council of Churches, the Churches Commission for Participation in Development and the Programme to Combat Racism, for example, were attempts to institutionalize this approach to development, the 'direct action' approach, rather than 'the formation of the Christian mind' approach.[9]

Many would, perhaps, still think in terms of forming the Christian mind first on such issues, and that has tremendous value, but if I were to leave a challenge with you, it might be this: if you were asked to take 'direct action' about a pressing issue of justice, local, national or international, how would you respond not only in terms of thought but of action?

'Work for the Lord with untiring effort and with great earnestness of spirit.' (Rom. 12.11)

— 5 —

Communion and Commission

*

—— Patterns of Partnership ——

I will begin by trying out a statement on my readers, 'The Churches of the Anglican Communion are churches of the Reformation'. Now it is true that the Anglican Reformers insisted on the continuity of the Anglican Church with the medieval and the early Church. The famous Archbishop Matthew Parker even insisted on going beyond the Mission of Augustine to discerning a continuity with the Celtic tradition of Christianity, and his work on the antiquity of the Church in *Britain*, not England, note, was an attempt to discern this continuity.[1] So there was a consciousness of continuity. Nevertheless, the Anglican Church at the time of the Reformation was manifestly a church of the Reformation, and it shared many of the characteristics of the other churches of the Reformation. One of them was an almost complete lack of a sense of mission. Now this is quite remarkable but it is almost universal in the churches of the Reformation, barring the Anabaptist tradition, and stands, of course, in sharp contrast to the great missionary efforts of the Counter Reformation in the Roman Catholic Church. There are of course several reasons given for this lack of a sense of mission in the churches of the Reformation.

There is, for example, a geographical point that is often made, that the sea routes at that time were controlled by either the Muslims or the Roman Catholic powers, and so it is said the churches of the Reformation had no opportunity to engage in world mission. Again, sometimes it is said that the relationship that many of the churches of the Reformation had with a particular people, a particular ethnic group, or a particular political dispensation, a state, for example, precluded interest beyond their doorstep or their shores. And when the Reformers themselves gave theological reasons for not engaging in mission, there was a curious kind of dispensationalism in operation, and it was often said that the great commission had been given only to the Apostles and that it did not apply in other ages!

But I am glad to say that there were exceptions to the rule and one such exception was Adrian Saravia. He was a Dutchman who became convinced of the necessity of episcopacy for the unity of the Church, and so he became an Anglican, there being no old Catholics at that time! He came to hold high office in the Church of England. Saravia fought against the general apathy towards mission at that time in the churches of the Reformation and particularly in the Church of England. One of the points that he made was that the promise of continuing communion with the risen Lord which occurs at the end of St Matthew's Gospel, where Jesus promises his disciples that he will be with them until the end of the age, goes hand in hand with the Great Commission, with going into all the world, preaching the gospel to all nations and baptizing them in the name of the Father and of the Son and of the Holy Spirit.[2] In other words, from the very beginning, communion and commission have gone together, and indeed we see that the writings that witness to the earliest period of the Church tell us that it was communion or fellowship with the Lord and among Christians that attracted people to the gospel, to the risen Christ as proclaimed by his disciples in fellowship together. This is already apparent in the second chapter of the Act of the Apostles, for example.

Now I would like to draw attention to the Epistle of Paul to the Philippians; it is a very important work as far as mission is concerned. We find at the very beginning of this Epistle that St Paul identifies the church at Philippi as sharing with him in the partnership of the gospel. *Koinonia eis to euangelion*: fellowship for the sake of the gospel. We could almost say, 'for the purpose of spreading the gospel'. They are partners (*sunkoinonoi*) with him in the defence (*apologia*) and confirmation (*bebaiosis*) of the gospel, they are partners with Paul. And so we find that *koinonia* (communion, fellowship) comes out strongly in terms of the mission of the Church and not only in terms of fellowship among believers. In the Acts of the Apostles and in the Pauline Epistles there seem to be different kinds of partnership in mission. First of all there is the inner circle of those whom Paul calls his fellow workers (*sunergoi*). There are numerous references in the New Testament to such people, but the most important are to be found right at the end of the Epistle to the Romans, in different parts of the Epistle to the Philippians, and in 1 Thessalonians. This was the inner circle of those who engaged in mission with Paul, who went with him on his missionary journeys perhaps, or who helped him in particular localities when he arrived there. Among this number there were women as well as men, slaves as well as free people.

The second kind of partnership that we can discern is the special partnership, with a supporting church, such as the one at Philippi. In other words, Paul and his companions look to support from particular local churches in the fulfilment of their worldwide mission. You will remember that Paul said at the end of the Epistle to the Philippians, that this church was the only one, at a particular stage in his career, that had partnership with him. All the others had turned away. He refers to the partnership as a 'giving and receiving,' so already at that early stage this is clear. And then, finally, there is the partnership between *churches* which Paul is seeking to build up. There is a long argument about this in the second Epistle to the Corinthians, and two whole chapters (8 and 9) are given to the development of this argument. Paul is arguing that just as the churches in Macedonia (and the church at Philippi was the chief among them) had forged a partnership with the churches in Judaea, so also the church in Corinth needs to forge a partnership with the Jewish Christians in Palestine. This partnership is based on the self-emptying love of Jesus Christ, who though he was rich, yet for our sakes, became poor. The churches should give not only out of their plenty but out of their want, and he praises the Macedonian churches in particular for giving out of their poverty. He goes on to argue that this partnership is for the sake of equality. Equality is not a fashionable word these days, but that is the word that Paul uses.

Now if I may comment: the mutual responsibility and interdependence processes that began in the Anglican Communion with the Congress in Toronto and which were later developed by the Anglican Consultative Council (ACC) in Dublin, set in train the Partners in Mission (PIM) movement, for instance.[3] These processes have emphasized this last aspect of partnership in mission, that is to say, the partnership between churches. This has been a very great blessing to the Anglican Communion, and if this is the only thing the ACC will ever achieve, it is enough! But it does not fully take into account the other kinds of partnership that we find in the New Testament: the enabling and support of individuals and voluntary bodies within the church where there is a specific vocation for mission. Having developed partnership between churches so well, I think it is now time that the Anglican Communion should give some attention to these other kinds of partnership.

In this connection I want to turn to the work of David Bosch. He reminds us in his book *Transforming Mission* of the distinction between *missionary* and *missionizing*. The whole Church is missionary by its very nature, and all Christians are called to commend the gospel by their style of life, to give an account of the hope that is in them. Once again that word *apologia* is used here in 1 Peter 3.15, and to welcome outsiders into their midst (Jas. 2.1–7). The whole Church is missionary but, says Bosch, there are special movements of people which are missionizing, fulfilling particular vocations that further God's mission in the world. All Christians should support such people, through giving and prayer, but above all by living in such a way that the Christian mission is seen as credible by outsiders.[4] There are many examples of such movements throughout the history of the Christian Church: think first of all of those wandering men and women in the early Church called prophets, who went from church to church bringing a particular charism, a particular ministry to each church. And what tremendous honour they were given there! They ranked, the *Didache* tells us, above the local presbyter-bishops. They could say the Eucharistic prayer extempore. Not even the Archbishop of Canterbury can do that!

Bishop Gore, in his work on the Christian ministry, which is still important, tells us that these prophets, as well as apostolic delegates and others, were prototypes for the historic episcopate when it emerged fully into the light. Gore was well aware that this prototype contained both men and women in the movement.[5] So there are the prophets, but then there is the emergence of monasticism, about which we can say that it is the single most influential factor in the spread of the gospel and of the church worldwide. Monasticism began in the East, in Egypt and in Syria and in what was then the Persian Empire. We find that in every Christian tradition monasticism has been important for mission.

We know in the West how monasticism not only helped to Christianize Europe, but also to civilize it and to save it from the ravages of the barbarians. But in the East also, the so-called 'Nestorian' Church, the Assyrian Church of the East, engaged in significant mission, which had lasting consequences in India, China, and in parts of central Asia, and it was the monks who took the gospel to these parts. The Coptic tradition has for long had a missionary concern and commitment to Africa which is natural, of course, because Egypt is part of Africa, and the Copts for a very long time worked and still continue to work in Ethiopia and on the Horn of Africa generally. As late as the nineteenth century the Ethiopian Copts were engaged in mission to Muslims and to people of primal religions in that part of the world (making many of the same mistakes that the Western missionaries were making a few hundred miles further East!)[6] So monasticism, movements of people called by God to particular vocations, has been used wonderfully in mission. Then there are lay movements, traders from Syria who spread the gospel and strengthened the Church in South India, or Russian Orthodox merchants who spread the gospel in the Far East.

In the Church of England itself, we see that in the eighteenth century, in the great ferment that appeared at that time, all sorts of voluntary movements of Christians emerged to fulfil particular tasks which they felt God was calling them to do. The struggle for the abolition of the slave trade and later of slavery itself, the struggle to improve the working conditions of men and women in Britain, to provide schools for the poor: all these were the result of voluntary movements, such as those resulting from the work of the Clapham Sect, in the Church of England, in the eighteenth and nineteenth centuries. The Church Missionary Society (CMS) was also a voluntary movement of this kind, and from the same kind of constituency. But before the CMS came into existence, the Society for the Propagation of the Gospel (SPG) and the Society for the Promotion of Christian Knowledge (SPCK) were also movements of people for spreading the gospel in different parts of the world. In the nineteenth century with the emergence of the Tractarian movement, we see the revival of religious communities in the Anglican communion, and they were a very significant factor in so many parts of the world, including of course, Southern Africa, in bringing the gospel to people, in planting the Church and in creating a lasting Christian witness.[7]

I want to plead for the importance of voluntary movements in the Church for the fulfilment of the Church's mission. The partnership between the churches can be greatly assisted by people who are called to fulfil particular tasks. The whole Church is missionary, but people are called to fulfil particular tasks in that missionary Church.

What is the role of the episcopate then in this context? I would say that it is recognizing, enabling, and directing voluntary movements in the Church, not controlling them. Recognizing what is a work of God in a particular place at a particular time, enabling that work, letting a thousand flowers bloom (if it's still permissible to quote Mao Tse Tung!) We need to think about directing people to where there is a need for the gospel. There is a need also for balance between canonical obedience to bishops and archbishops and the freedom to take initiatives. Obedience should not repress or suppress initiative. Look at Paul and his companions; they reported back regularly to the church that sent them and yet they were able in the middle of all of that to respond to the promptings of the Holy Spirit, sometimes in quite radical ways, like taking the gospel to Europe!

53

If these different patterns of partnership in mission are going to be taken seriously, they will need to be embodied in the life of the churches. And we find that this is precisely what is happening. This is very encouraging. For example, in the Church of England, we have recently taken a step which brings together the voluntary mission agencies and representatives of General Synod into fellowship with each other in a common committee which is answerable to the Church of England as a whole, and which belongs to the structures of the Church of England. Such a structure now needs to be reflected in diocesan and parochial life and, perhaps, in the life of General Synod itself.

Some years ago I was invited by the Episcopal Church in the USA to attend a consultation to consider how their unit for World Mission could relate to the many voluntary movements that were coming into being in the Episcopal Church. As a result of that consultation, I believe, they arrived at some kind of arrangement which facilitates dialogue between the two sides. In Tanzania, the Anglican Evangelistic Association has a particular relationship with the province. The Mar Thoma Syrian Church, a church with which we are in full communion, has its Evangelistic Association which has carried out pioneering missionary work in Nepal and Tibet and many other parts of the world. The Church of South India, a united church in full communion, has the Indian Missionary Society which they support.

At the last meeting of MISAG – the Mission Issues Strategy and Advisory Group – (and by the last meeting I mean the very last, because there aren't going to be any more MISAG meetings), a recommendation was made that there should be a standing commission on mission in the Anglican Communion, which we provisionally named MISSIO. This should have within it representatives from provinces in the 'North' and the 'South' and representatives from mission agencies and other voluntary movements in the 'North' and the 'South', because we found that in many 'Southern' contexts too God was raising up people to fulfil particular tasks and we wished to encourage this. MISAG'S recommendations were approved at the joint meeting of the Primates of the Anglican Communion and the Anglican Consultative Council. It is very important that the balance of representation suggested by MISAG be maintained.[8]

—— Modes of Mission ——

Coming now to modes of mission; first of all, there is *roaming*. One remembers the 'go' of the Great Commission, 'go into the world . . .'

Now this 'go' is usually read as an imperative: 'you *should* go', 'you *have* to go', etc., but my reading of the text suggests that it needn't be because it could be translated '*having gone* . . . disciples of all nations' (Matt. 28.19). In the early Church, people often found themselves in a place not because they had gone there intentionally but because they had been displaced by harassment or persecution (e.g. Acts 11.19f). Such displacements have always been significant for mission. It is certainly true that more and more people are finding themselves in a particular place not intentionally, but because that is the way it has happened. We need to consider here the significance of the displacement of people on a large scale in today's world. There are refugees in so many different parts of the world, and these refugees have a particular significance, I believe, for the Church. When, as a result of the tyranny of Idi Amin, some Ugandans had to flee to Zaire, the result was a great strengthening of the Church in Zaire.

In the Sudan, we find that despite the great displacement of people, and perhaps because of it, the Church has grown tremendously in particular parts of that country, and indeed, in neighbouring countries. In other parts of the world the displacement of people has meant that the Church can now minister to people to whom it had no access in the past. Think of the Somali refugees in Northern Kenya, for example, or of the hundreds of thousands of Iranis in the cities in Australia, in Melbourne, and in Sydney, and also in New York, Los Angeles and London.

But although the displacement of people in this way is significant for mission, there is also an intentional 'going'. Returning to Archbishop Parker's tracing of the continuity of the Anglican Church with the Church of the Celts we find that 'roaming' was a fundamental aspect of Celtic Christianity, it had to do with their make up. They roamed, of course, for different reasons, but as they roamed, they began to realize that this roaming was significant for mission, and gradually the roaming became intentional as far as mission was concerned. So we have the great stories of the evangelization of Northern Britain by people like Columba, of the missionary work of Columbanus in continental Europe, of Aidan and Chad and of the establishment of Iona and Lindisfarne as centres of mission. We have to be prepared to go with the gospel, ready to meet Christ when we arrive. The roaming of the Celtic saints was not aimless, it was not hit and run, they established important centres for the nurture of those they evangelized. It was directed and committed.[9]

So 'roaming' leads to '*remaining*', to the establishment of Holy Island and to the nurture of people who would take over leadership in the churches which had been established. And if roaming is the Celtic paradigm, remaining is the Augustinian one. Gregory's charge to Augustine, when he was sent out rather reluctantly to England on his mission, was to take the culture of the local people seriously, not needlessly to destroy what he found there, but somehow to transform it by the proclamation of the Gospel.[10] And it was this charge, I believe, that is at the root of the Anglican commitment to incarnation that has been mentioned so many times already. We find that one expression of this commitment was the creation of the parochial system under Theodore of Tarsus.

But it is not only Anglicans or the Church in England or Britain that was and is committed to incarnation. The Franciscans on the continent of Europe, for example, had a very well-developed and sophisticated view of incarnational presence, particularly in relation to mission to Muslims. One remembers that they were among the first to advocate a peaceful approach to Islam.[11] Their view was that at first, and sometimes for a long time afterwards, all Christians need to do is to go and live in a particular place, a particular culture, among a particular people, to learn their ways, to hear their stories, to live as Christians, to minister to people's needs and to discern the right time, the *kairos*, for the proclamation of the gospel. Now that may take centuries or a few years, or only a few days, but they distinguished between presence and proclamation and it is still right of course to do that.[12]

Presence should result in *penetration* of culture. Presence can be alienating, if, for instance, the church in a particular place represents one class interest over others. Then the other classes will be alienated. I remember a priest in the Church of England who came from the East End of London saying that when he announced to his family that he had a vocation to the ministerial priesthood, he was regarded as a traitor, because this was seen as class treachery! Choices in terms of liturgy, music, and even the physical arrangements of a church can attract or alienate people from the church. And so presence needs to be more than presence, it needs to come to grips with the world view, the beliefs, and the values of the people where the church is present. It has to identify as well as to be present, and in this connection we find that the first Inter-Anglican Theological and Doctrinal Commission that was chaired by Archbishop Keith Rayner did some valuable work when it pointed out that although the Anglican Reformers regarded reason as a universal human faculty which was the same in every culture and among every people, in fact we now know this is not the case.

Because of our shared humanity there is a great deal in common among cultures; still, every culture has its world view, its values and its beliefs, and it is the glory of the gospel that it can appeal to the world view, the beliefs, and the values of each culture. It is these that constitute the 'reason' of every culture, and the gospel has to find 'hooks' into this reason.[13] I find this re-interpretation of reason in the Anglican triad of Scripture, Tradition and Reason very attractive indeed. Now, of course, this is not just wishful thinking. As a matter of fact, during the course of history this is precisely what has happened: the gospel has actually appealed to many diverse world views, values and beliefs. And so we find that we reach a stage when the gospel so permeates a culture, influences it, so materially, if you like, that a whole people can call themselves Christian. National or *popular* churches, in other words, come into being. Armenia was the first nation to call itself Christian, and there was a Christendom in Ethiopia before there was a Christendom in Western Europe. Then there are the Georgians, the Copts and so many others whose cultures were so permeated with the gospel that national churches came into existence.[14]

Now a church can be national without being established. The Roman Catholic Church in France, for example, is clearly the national church of France but it is certainly not, at least since the revolution, established. And then there might be different kinds of establishment: the Church of Scotland is established, but the nature of its establishment is rather different from the establishment of the Church of England. If establishment is seen as a desire by the people of a nation to give a place to the Church in the decision-making structures of the state, it may be acceptable. Such an arrangement would also allow the organs of state to have some say in the affairs of the Church. But this should not compromise the gospel nor result in a weakening of the Church as the body of Christ where believers are strengthened for mission. Of course, the Church should not be a sect and should be open to people of all kinds, committed and uncommitted. The Church should also be open to advice and criticism from all sides. But that does not mean that the uncommitted and the casual visitor should have a *determinative* say in the affairs of the Church. If that begins to happen, then we are going in the direction of compromise and the loss of a sense of purpose. Archbishop Michael Ramsey rightly believed that the Church must have control over its own doctrine and worship (and one might add appointments) while remaining open to the participation in its councils of people drawn from across the spectrum of national life. Such people should be able to *influence* but not to *determine* the church's priorities in the fulfilment of its task.

Now while the gospel has an attachment point (*anknüpfungspunkt* is a word that Emil Brunner used) with every culture, a proper estimate of the doctrine of the Fall also leads us to the view that the gospel, not the Church, judges aspects of cultures, their world views and customs. This critical principle is found already in the capacity of the Old Testament prophets to oppose corruption, oppression, and idolatry in contemporary Israelite culture, including its religious aspect. This is why I say that it must be the gospel, the word of God, and not the Church that judges. We find that this *prophetic* work is continued in the ministry of Jesus and in the life of the early Church, in the opposition to emperor worship, for example. Charles Elliot, who used to work for Christian Aid, relates the contemporary Christian concern regarding structural injustice and social sin to the rediscovery of the centrality of themes such as justice and mercy in the biblical witness.[15] I don't need to underline that in South Africa this prophetic ministry of the Church has been recognized by international and national leadership. But there are examples from other parts of the Anglican communion, such as East Africa, where the Church was the first to speak out against an unjust government.

In liberation theology from South America, this prophetic witness is brought to bear on the Church as well as the world, as the Church is seen as implicated in the oppression. In additon to the *popular* and the *prophetic* there is the witness of the *persecuted* church. Although the persecution of the Church under Marxist regimes has disappeared or is disappearing, we find that the Church is being persecuted in other parts of the world by other kinds of people, and this needs to be taken seriously by the Anglican communion, because, not only are these fellow Christians but many of them are fellow Anglicans. As I have noted in relation to the Sudan, persecution often results in great blessing for the Church. The blood of the martyrs is indeed the seed of the Church. This witness of the persecuted church, the world hears and we need to hear.

The whole of Christian mission, however it is exercised, pre-supposes *dialogue* and depends upon it. There can be no Christian mission without dialogue, as dialogue is the basis for all human community. Communities have dialogue internally: how to order themselves on questions of law and order and justice, for instance, or on matters such as the distribution of resources. Communities also have dialogue with each other about fair trade, for example, or about the need for peace. And so the Church too finds itself engaged in dialogue on a whole number of fronts. What then is the scope of the Church's dialogue? We have noted already the dialogue with cultural values and beliefs. The representative from the Democratic Party in

South Africa said that the basis for his party's actions was a belief in the innate dignity of all human beings. The Church's dialogue with such belief, which is widespread, needs to ask what is the basis for this belief in the innate dignity of human beings? Here the Church may have something to say! Dialogue with the scientific community: what is the basis for that intelligibility of the world by the human mind which makes science itself possible? Dialogue with those in the arts: George Steiner wrote that all art is concerned with transcendence. If that is so, what is the Church doing about it? In fact he goes further and says that all post-war European art is concerned with only one question: the presence or the absence of God! And then there is the dialogue with people of other faiths and ideologies: is there a common spiritual quest in which we are all engaged? If so, what is the unique Christian contribution to this?[16]

What is the theological basis for the Church's dialogue? I want only to mention three points: the first, the *imago Dei*, the image of God in all human beings, which is certainly affected and spoilt by sin, but not destroyed by it. The Church can address humanity, can address human groups and cultures, because of the surviving image of God in them. And then there is the presence of the *Logos*, the light of the eternal Word in all human beings that St John talks about in his prologue to the Gospel. This, of course, was picked up by some of the early Fathers, by Justin Martyr and Clement of Alexandria in particular, in their idea of the *Logos Spermatikos*. They saw the work of the divine Logos especially in the *philosophy* of their pagan context, in the *practical morality* of the Stoics and even in the *prophecies* of the oracles. There is a foretaste of this in Paul's speech at Athens (Acts 17). And then, of course, there is the presence and work of the Holy Spirit in the world, and not only in the Church. Once again the Johannine writings alert us to this: the Spirit bringing the world to a knowledge of righteousness and of sin and of judgement. This 'economy' of the Holy Spirit plays an important part in an orthodox understanding of our relations with those of other faiths. The basis for dialogue is thus shown to have a Trinitarian structure, and reminds us of the communicating God of the Bible.

Now dialogue can be practised in a whole number of ways: there is for instance, *discursive* dialogue, where the parties exchange information about themselves and their beliefs. Then there is *interior* dialogue, where people talk about their spiritual experiences, and each attempts to understand the other's. There is also dialogue for the building up of a *community* in which the different sides live, and dialogue about the recognition of our *common humanity*. Today, there is much dialogue about how the different faiths view the *environment* and how we can gain insights about the right relationship with our environment from the different traditions. There is also the dialogue which involves *common study* of a particular issue or belief with a view to removing misunderstandings and clarifying matters.[17]

Some people say that dialogue is all very well, but it is not enough. These are the advocates of *direct action*. As we have seen, they have had their supporters throughout Christian history: the ransoming of slaves, the visiting of those in prison, going to the disreputable parts of the cities in the ancient world to minister to the poor, the long-term educational and medical commitment of the churches, and today the provision of relief and longer-term community-based development and service to the poor, all depend on such 'activist' views. But there are some who say even that is not enough. These are the people who argue for direct action in terms of participation in *social struggle* to secure justice in society, and some World Council of Churches programmes have taken this on board. The Programme to Combat Racism (PCR) and the Commission on the Churches' Participation in Development (CCPD) are actually based on the philosophy of such direct action, where *community* and solidarity is to be found with the poor, so as to take their side in the *conflict* which must precede the securing of justice for them, in their *conscientization* which enables them to organize and in their liberation which enables them to be *co-creators* of their own future. Co-creators, of course, with God.

As we engage in different kinds of mission and in different ways, we find that we come to a point where we need to *declare* the good news of Jesus Christ. In fact as we engage in mission in its different ways, we find that declaration is an aspect of each of these ways. It is not an accident that *kerysso* and *kerygma* are related words in the Bible. In other words, the meaning of the gospel is disclosed in its proclamation! We are called to challenge people through word and act and attitude, to consider the claims of Christ, to invite them to follow him, and to nurture them in the Faith.

— 6 —

Mission and Unity:
Thinking Globally, Acting Locally

✳

I am not, I must confess at the outset, an 'ecumaniac' because I think to go forward in ecumenism today one has to be a realist. People are speaking nowadays quite freely of the winter of ecumenism. It may not be a winter but it is certainly an autumn, and there are many discouragements on every side. I shall refer to some in the course of this chapter, and I think that we need hard-headed commitment, to put our heads down, as it were, and to get on with the difficult tasks that ecumenism today is setting us.

The Edinburgh Conference of 1910 was the focus for, and the culmination of, several decades, if not centuries, of ecumenical interaction. But what *are* the origins of the ecumenical movement?

—— Breaking down Barriers ——

It is difficult to know where to begin, but I suppose we could begin with the Evangelical Revival in the eighteenth century which began to break down barriers of denomination: as people were caught up in the revival, they began to cross denominational frontiers. Think, for example, of Wesley's heart being warmed and his conversion at a Moravian meeting. Denominations became less and less important and, in a very real way, the witness of Methodism showed people back in the eighteenth century how it was possible to belong to more than one group of Christians. This evangelical revival had very important results.

For example, it brought about the beginnings of a consciousness of world mission and this resulted in the formation of interdenominational mission agencies, such as the London Missionary Society which was established as early as 1795. But even when denominational agencies, like the Church Missionary Society, came into existence and the Society for the Propagation of the Gospel (which later became USPG) before it, they were happy to use Christians from other churches in their work.[1] In fact, CMS could not have begun its work if it had not been able to use people from Germany, and some of its most distinguished missionaries in the early days were Lutherans from the Evangelical Lutheran Church of Württemberg.[2]

Similarly, SPCK and USPG used people from Germany and Denmark for a very long time in their work, sometimes as chaplains and therefore functioning in an ordained capacity. Some of these people were reordained by Anglican bishops, but some were not.[3] Apart from mission agencies, there was also the work of the Bible Society, for example, which encouraged Christians of different traditions to work together.

As world mission got under way in the nineteenth century, we find arrangements of comity, as they were called, between different denominations so that not too many denominations were to be found working in any one area. Now this arrangement of comity did not always work, but there was goodwill for it nonetheless.

Again in the eighteenth century, on the other side, as it were, you have the Nonjurors in the Church of England: those people who for reasons of conscience were unable to take the oath of allegiance to William and Mary because they had taken one to James. For that reason they were deprived of their livings and of their sees (there were nine bishops among the Nonjurors), and formed a kind of Anglican community that was not quite a Church but had ecclesial dimensions.

—— *Ecumenical Contact* ——

They began very serious contact with Eastern Orthodoxy. This contact was prolonged, it influenced the liturgy of the Nonjurors to a very great extent, and this liturgy influenced the liturgy of the Scottish Episcopal Church, which in turn influenced liturgies in different parts of the Anglican Communion, including the USA. That was another kind of ecumenical contact. Although in the end these negotiations were abortive – they did not result in full ecclesial communion – nevertheless they are very significant.[4]

Then, early in the nineteenth century, CMS decided to respond to a request by the Ancient Oriental Church in India for theological teachers, because that Church wanted to renew its life and, to do so, it felt that it needed to train priests in a new way. Once again, this resulted in ecumenical contact. There was a great deal of heartache about this because, of course, CMS being what it was, and although determined not to proselytize, did create a certain kind of temper in the priests who were being trained by CMS missionaries and, in the end, this sadly resulted in a schism in the Ancient Oriental Church in India and the coming into being of the Mar Thoma Church.[5]

However, I just want to point out that this kind of contact was already established in the early nineteenth century. Throughout that century, Anglicans maintained contact with the Ancient Oriental Churches in the Middle East and India. The Archbishop of Canterbury's Mission to the Assyrians, for example, is another instance of this, and to this day the Ancient Oriental Churches in the East have some respect for the Anglican Communion because no attempt was made to proselytize, and the mission to the Assyrians and the mission to the Indians were both seen as a service to the Church.[6]

So, when the conference took place in Edinburgh in 1910, delegates were faced with nearly two hundred years of existing ecumenical contact of one kind or another. They had before them two problems, and these problems have been with the ecumenical movement ever since.

—— Local Christian Disunity ——

One was the problem of Christian disunity locally, the perception by the people at Edinburgh that Christian disunity at the local level was destructive for Christian mission at the local level.

As Father, now Bishop, Duprey of the Vatican said at the 1988 Lambeth Conference, what can a divided church offer a divided world? When people see that Christians are not united among themselves, this casts doubt on the gospel of God's reconciling love in Christ which they seek to proclaim. This was a problem because, despite comity arrangements, there were many situations where Christians were competing for converts.

—— Creating World Structures ——

The other problem had to do with the creation of world structures that would carry the ecumenical movement forward. Now, the Edinburgh conference was actually quite successful in this because, soon afterwards, both the International Missionary Council and the Faith and Order Movement came into being. Both had important ecumenical consequences in the emergence later on of the World Council of Churches.[7]

At the same time within the Anglican Communion there was, towards the close of the nineteenth century, the Lambeth Quadrilateral, which has its origin in the Episcopal Church in the USA, but which was accepted by the bishops at the Lambeth Conference of 1888 as a way by which Anglicans could accept unity with other Christians. The provisions of the Quadrilateral have to do with a mutual acceptance of the authority of Scripture, of the sacraments instituted by Christ himself, of the historic creeds and of the historic ministry.[8]

Then, in 1920, another Lambeth Conference issued the famous appeal to all Christian people. This appeal had important results. For the first time it created a dialogue, however informal, between the Roman Catholic Church and Anglicans, and it also began a series of conversations between Anglicans and Free Churches, these conversations resulting, among other things, in the eventual creation of the Church of South India.[9]

—— Common Witness and Convergence ——

That, as it were, is the history. During the course of the ecumenical movement, certain things have become *common* to Christians everywhere and on certain matters we have *converged*. I would like to draw attention to the things which are common and where the convergences are.

First, the common things. It has become possible for Christians of different kinds to make a *common witness* on issues. Christians have been quite effective in a common witness against great social evils – racial discrimination, for example, in the United States and in a more pronounced form in South Africa. The struggle against apartheid was led by the churches, and by the churches *together*.

Christians have been able to make a common witness against policies that are unjust to immigrants or refugees, for example. Christians have been able to take a common stance on certain kinds of aggression against weaker peoples and countries. They have taken common positions on fair international trade and the question of debt. It is a delight for me to work as a member of the Board of Christian Aid, where there is substantial agreement among Christians on what to do about world development. Now we take this for granted, but the existence of Christian Aid itself is quite special; such bodies do not exist in every country. In the United States, for example, although the National Council of Churches there has a programme, each church has its own programme of aid and development as well. And so, for Christian Aid to exist as an ecumenical body, through which the churches can act in these areas, is a great strength for the churches and for the cause.

A common witness has been possible then in areas of social morality, but it has not been so easy on questions of personal and family morality, and here we might say that this area has more to do with the need for convergence than with a common witness.

Most Christians, I think, have common norms: a respect for life, for example; an understanding of the seriousness of marriage, an understanding that marriage has to do with family. Yet the particular conclusions that they draw from these general norms have been very different and, as technology poses us newer problems, my guess is that there will be greater divergence among churches and Christians rather than convergence. This will pose a quite serious ecumenical problem to which we should be giving our attention.

—— *The Confession of a Common Faith* ——

Let us move on from common witness to the *confession of a common faith*. In many ecumenical services and meetings it is possible for Christians to make a common confession of faith. The World Council of Churches is itself founded on a common confession of faith in the Holy Trinity as revealed in Scripture. The Faith and Order Commission of the World Council of Churches has recently issued a document which is called *Confessing the One Faith*. It has taken ten years for them to put this document together, not because they have been lazy but because it has been so difficult. This document is a tremendous reassurance to Christians that they really believe the same things together.[10]

It is not good enough for people who want to divide Christians to say 'Ah, because you believe in the ordination of women, you must believe in a different sort of Christ to the one another group of Christians believe in'. A common confession of faith will do away with this kind of recrimination and criticism both from outside and among Christians.

—— *Common Prayer and Worship* ——

Then there is the reality of *common prayer and worship* together. Some time ago, I was in a procession in Notre Dame with the Archbishop of Paris. As we processed, I thought to myself this would not have happened forty years ago. Yet we were welcomed, we were given a place in the sanctuary, we prayed together, an Anglican member read one of the lessons at the Eucharist and so on. Now, of course, it is possible for us to pray together but there still remains the pain of not being able to do everything together (we were not able to communicate that evening). Nevertheless, a great deal of common prayer has become possible for Christians of all kinds and we need to be deeply grateful to God for this. 'In the one Spirit we were all baptised . . . and the one Spirit was given to us all to drink' (1 Cor. 12.13).

——— Convergence and Communion ———

In some areas, then, Christians have common attitudes but, in other matters, while they have not yet attained a common mind, there are important *convergences*.

I think that the most important convergence, the paradigmatic convergence, has taken place in the way in which we now speak of the Church, and the fundamental category in our language about the Church has become that of *communion*: communion between the churches, among the churches, and communion among Christians within a local church. We have become very used to this, but we must remind ourselves of what existed before. At least in some parts of the Christian world, it is no longer possible to say that being part of the Church of Christ has to do with being in communion with one man somewhere or other, wherever that may be. Communion between the Churches has to do with sacramental, ministerial, and supportive relationships between local churches in different parts of the world.

In the same way, communion within a local fellowship has to do not so much with the ministry of one person, usually a man, but with relationships, a nexus of relationships, among Christians in a local place. However untidy it is, that is what communion is about. Communion is not about tidiness, it is not about logic, it is not about textbooks on dogmatics, it is about the living reality of Christians living together, worshipping together, serving together. So communion has become a basic category in which to talk and to think.[11]

——— The Ordained Ministry ———

Naturally, this raises questions about the place of the ordained ministry. What is the place of the ordained ministry in the service of such a communion of churches? First, it is very encouraging to note that nearly all the churches in the world now acknowledge the priesthood of all believers, that the laity genuinely have an apostolate to fulfil, that the laity are called by God to mission in the world, and it is a mission that is crucial for the Church and for the world.

The ordained ministry, then, is called to serve the unity of Christians in a particular place, in a particular country, or, indeed, in the whole world. Now we may ask what sort of ministry, and certain ecumenical documents like *Baptism, Eucharist and Ministry*, the so-called Lima document, now tell us how much agreement is possible even about that.[12]

Whatever claims people might make about the threefold order of bishop, priest and deacon, it is at the very least an ancient and agreeable way of ordering the Church. 'Lima' is agreed about that, many ecumenical conversations have come to an agreement about that, and while, on the one hand, there is agreement that the laity have a priesthood, there is also agreement that the ordained ministry needs certain charisms, certain gifts, certain graces, if that ministry is to carry out its service of unity. This is very remarkable agreement on some very important matters.

—— *A Focus of Unity* ——

Where Anglicans are concerned and, indeed, where all those having an episcopal system of government are concerned, I think it is right to say that if we acknowledge the need for a focus of unity at the local level, which we would if we had an episcopal system of government, then, logically, we are bound to accept a focus of unity at the universal level, and there has been, once again, significant convergence of views about the ministry of the Bishop of Rome.

Of course, a universal primate need not necessarily be the Bishop of Rome, we could invent one, but there are arguments for agreeing that the Bishop of Rome has had in the past, and should have in the future, a significant ministry of focusing the unity of the world-wide Church. Whether that becomes a reality depends on the behaviour not only of ordinary Christians of different kinds but on the behaviour of the Bishop of Rome himself.[13]

—— *Holy Scripture* ——

Then, I am very encouraged to note that in the ecumenical dialogues there has been quite significant convergence on the place of *holy Scripture*. If you read the reports of these dialogues, again and again they refer to the normative character of the records of holy Scripture.

Now, this is not to be understood in a fundamentalist way, because these dialogues also recognize that behind holy Scripture lie very long oral traditions which have given rise to Scripture. After Scripture had been recognized as such by the Church, there came into being traditions of interpreting it and any statement about the place of Scripture in the Church must take such traditions into account.

We do not have agreement yet but only convergence, because some people continue to use Scripture in a fundamentalist way, in a way that does not take into account a historical, critical understanding of Scripture. In other words, they tend to want to read out of Scripture, just like that, an understanding of the structures in their Church, for example. And they may even say that what their Church teaches is, by its very nature, consonant with Scripture rather than such teaching having to be shown to be consonant.

This is, I think, a very important and fundamental divide in ecumenical conversations between those who claim that their judgements about matters of faith or behaviour are in accordance with Scripture *because* they are *their* statements, and those who demand to be shown *how* such statements are consonant with Scripture.

There is another divide, and that is between those churches which accept the possibility of development in Christian belief and doctrine and those churches which do not, which place such a high store by Scripture and tradition that they are not willing to see that there may be authentic development. Both these problems one comes across in ecumenical dialogue sooner or later.

—— *Baptism* ——

There has been very significant convergence in our views on the *sacraments* – baptism, for example. The Lima document makes it quite clear that Christians of different kinds are beginning to recognize the baptism of other Christians. This is not without problems but some movement is beginning to take place. Those who baptize only those who have made a profession of faith are beginning to see why others baptize infants. Those who baptize infants are beginning to see why profession of faith is such a serious matter for baptism.[14]

Now I am bound to say that I sympathize very much with the warnings of 'Lima' about indiscriminate baptism, where those churches are concerned which baptize infants. Somebody said to me, 'Nobody has an indiscriminate policy of baptism, however open their policy.' Well, if that is so, that is excellent. But those churches which *do* baptize infants, need to consider very seriously how the children they baptize are to be nurtured in the faith.

I am quite aware that it is not possible to place this burden on parents on all occasions, that the congregation has to play a more significant role, that the sponsors have to be very carefully chosen. However we do it, we must, when we baptize infants, have a reasonable expectation that the child will be given Christian nurture, and I think the Lima document is right in implying that those who do not do this, if there are any such, are behaving less than responsibly.

I do not know what sort of comment that is on the recent General Synod debate and its outcome, but I was interested to see that the International Anglican Consultation on the Liturgy, which happened quite soon after that debate, echoed the Lima document in this matter, and I think that is significant. But there has been tremendous convergence in our thinking about baptism.

—— *The Eucharist and Anamnesis* ——

Where the Eucharist is concerned, once again the great achievement of ecumenical conversation has been to make it possible for all churches and all Christians to talk of the real presence of Christ in the Eucharist. Some Christians talked as if there was a real absence!

But it has become possible to talk of the real presence of Christ, as it is taught in Scripture, largely because of the work of biblical scholars. We have a better understanding now of what Christ might have meant when he said 'Do this in my remembrance'. Some people say that too much weight is put on that word *anamnesis*, but, as far as I can see, in the Old Testament and in the New it must mean more than simply being a memorial in the sense that we use that word.

In the Old Testament, it echoes a word that has to do with calling to the present an event in the past, of making actual in the present an event of the past; it has to do, for example, with the Passover ritual. Each Passover is *the* Passover, it is not simply a memorial of the Passover. That is the power of the Passover festival! When you think of the grounding of the Christian Eucharist in the Passover, you can begin to appreciate what *anamnesis* actually means.

Now, of course, there are some who declare that it is not enough to say that Christ is truly present in the Eucharist, you must say *how* he is present, and these are the people who want us to return to the old scholastic and sterile debates about the way in which Christ is present. My fear is that we shall hear more from such people, not less, in the immediate future. That is sad because many eminent theologians in the Roman Catholic Church, for example, have done enormously useful work on making possible a contemporary understanding of the presence of Christ in the Eucharist. Think of Father Schillebeeckx's work on transignification.[15]

Ecumenical dialogue on the Eucharist will only go forward if we all accept that Christ is truly present, but do not press our brothers and sisters to say what, in the end, is mystery, what cannot be said, and especially not press them to say things in ways that modern people can hardly understand.

—— The Four Marks ——

So in these areas there has been convergence. As I have said, the Anglican Communion itself was quite prophetic when, in 1888, the Lambeth Quadrilateral was accepted by the bishops gathered together in a Lambeth Conference. It was quite courageous to say at that time that Anglicans were prepared to unite with Christians who could accept those four marks of the Christian life – the authority of Scripture, the sacraments, the historic creeds and the historic ministry. Now we find that ecumenical agreements like *Baptism, Eucharist and Ministry* are moving towards a position like that of the Lambeth Quadrilateral: the acceptance of the historic ministry, the acceptance of the Eucharist and baptism as sacraments instituted by Christ himself.

The new document *Confessing the One Faith* recognizes how the historic creeds are valuable for Christians in expressing their faith, not simply by way of repetition but as setting for us the parameters for our discussion on belief. All this has become possible. The place of Holy Scripture has been discussed, and there is some understanding about how Scripture is to be used.

But at the very time, and this is paradoxical, that the ecumenical movement is moving towards a recognition of the conditions of the Lambeth Quadrilateral, the Anglican Communion is getting cold feet. It is moving back into a denominational, and almost a sectarian, mood.

—— Denominational Politics ——

I was speaking to a prominent official of the World Council of Churches once who said the days for church unions, like the Church of South India union, have now gone. Why have they gone? The reason has not to do with theology, the reason has not to do with people's faith or their devotion, the reason has to do with denominational politics.

Again and again, church union schemes in different parts of the world, including this country, have failed for political reasons rather than strictly doctrinal, theological reasons. So I am not sure that we can say that the day for church unions of that kind has gone. But it is certainly true that Anglicans, as they draw back from a commitment to unity on the basis of the Quadrilateral, are drawing back for all sorts of reasons having to do with 'character' and 'identity' rather than reasons of doctrinal or sacramental theology.

Now, of course, character and identity are important things, but an appeal to them can disguise prejudice. It can hide a desire not to change, and I am quite alarmed when people, watching five hundred bishops process through Canterbury Cathedral, say, 'This is Anglicanism'. That can very easily become idolatry.

The fundamental documents of Anglicanism make it radically provisional in character and allow for the church in each culture, each place, to express its Christian faith in its own way, while remaining in fellowship with the worldwide Church. This is a valuable witness that Anglicanism must bring to the world Church at this time rather than retreating into narrow denominationalism.

—— *Unity and Catholicity* ——

One fear that is sometimes expressed, particularly where union with Nonconformist churches is concerned, has to do with the apprehension that, somehow, such a unity would make the Church 'less catholic'. This is a criticism that was made of the Church of South India, when it came into being. I find this very difficult to understand, and Roman Catholic colleagues with whom I have spoken have also found it difficult to understand. What makes the Church less or more catholic, or sufficiently catholic, whatever that is, is how Christians come to be in unity, not that they *are* in unity, and my hope would be that any union in which Anglicans are involved is in fidelity to apostolic faith and practice as Anglicans have inherited it, and as they have reflected on it.

Now, admittedly, they themselves have not been faithful to it in many cases, and there is a need for repentance, but to say that union will make a Church less catholic is to have little faith in God. It is God who, by his grace in the sacraments, in the reading of the Scriptures, and in the ministerial priesthood, gives the Church grace to be catholic, sufficiently catholic, adequately catholic.

——— *Local Ecumenical Projects* ———

As to reflection on how such unions are to go forward in the future, I believe that the existence of local ecumenical projects is providential for the Church in this country, but not only for the Church in this country, for the Church in the world. I was talking to someone in Geneva, in the World Council of Churches, and asked him about local ecumenical projects elsewhere. As we discussed the matter, it became clear to me that it is very difficult to find exact parallels elsewhere for the sort of ecumenical projects which exist here.

There are, of course, different ways in which people co-operate ecumenically, but the emergence of united churches, uniting churches, whatever you want to call them, in local settings in this country is a very great advance and should not be underestimated. I believe that they do lack something, and that is a national voice. If the local ecumenical projects are to have an impact on national churches and, indeed, the world Church, there must be some forum where their voices together can be heard. So I would hope that the Group for Local Unity (GLU) will provide such a voice.

——— *Dialogue with Other Faiths* ———

The catholicity of the Church is not a static concept, of course. Catholicity is not only about communion among the churches, it is not only about communion among local Christians. Catholicity has to do with the whole world, the whole *oikoumene*, the whole of the inhabited world, and for this reason it is absolutely essential that ecumenism should be in a close relationship to dialogue with people outside the Christian churches (with people of other faiths, for example).

Now, I am not sure of expressions like 'the wider ecumenism'. I think it is perhaps wiser to keep the term ecumenism to conversations among Christians but, having said that, the Church cannot be catholic until it is in a relationship of dialogue and of mission to the rest of the world.

The American Episcopalian theologian John Knox said about the Church that it is an ever-widening sphere of an ever-deepening reconciliation. If the Church is that, if that is the calling of the Church, then the Church must always be in dialogue with the community, with people of other faiths and with all those of goodwill.[16]

— PART TWO —

Dialogue

— 7 —

Dialogue in an Age
of Conflict

※

We have seen that dialogue is an aspect of the human condition and, in fact, all human societies presuppose a certain amount of encounter and of dialogue as the basis for their existence; 'as iron sharpeneth iron so the countenance of man his fellow', as the Bible says (Prov. 27.17). We should not forget that today there are different ways in which communities and people continue to have dialogue with one another. There is, for example, dialogue which is *internal* to a society; how laws should be made, how a society is to be defended against its enemies, what will ensure a society's prosperity. At the same time there is dialogue *between* communites; how to promote trade, for example, or keep the peace, or plan together for scientific research.

—— The Scope of Dialogue ——

The Church too is engaged in dialogue on a number of fronts, and its dialogue is not limited to that with people of other faiths. For example, the Church is and should be involved in dialogue with the scientific community about religious beliefs and the ever-changing perceptions of science, and how the one relates to the other. The Church needs to be in dialogue with the arts and the ways in which perceptions of transcendence are appreciated by artists. A very significant book on this by George Steiner called *Real Presences* shows us the importance of dialogue with those in the arts; Steiner believes that all art raises profound issues regarding religion.[1] If this is true, it provides an important basis for dialogue between the Church and the arts. So as we talk about dialogue with people of other faiths, this has to be put in the context of the Church's call to dialogue with the world in its several manifestations.

On what is the Church's dialogue based? It is based first of all on the recognition that men and women everywhere are created in the image of God (Gen. 1.27). It is true that this image has to some extent been affected by human sin, both communal and personal, but nevertheless the image survives, it has not been destroyed and we have dialogue with people who are not Christians, because we believe this image is there and that this image has something of God, both in communities and within individuals. Second, we recognize that the Eternal Word, the Logos, incarnate in Jesus Christ, has illuminated all human beings everywhere, as St John tells us clearly at the beginning of his Gospel (John 1.4, 9). We saw that this recognition of the universal illumination of the Eternal Word was present in some of the early Fathers of the Church, in Justin Martyr and Clement of Alexandria, for example, who believed that some of the greatest achievements of their particular civilization, Stoic and Platonist philosophy, for example, were possible because of the presence of the divine Word in them. At the same time, we need to note that Justin and Clement were much more reserved about the presence of the Eternal Word in certain, contemporary religious expressions of the time.[2] Now the presence and illumination of the divine Word in human societies and individuals is obscured by human sin, and although we recognize its presence we also recognize the obscuring and distorting effects of human sin. Then third, we base our dialogue on the presence and work of God's Holy Spirit in the world and not merely in the Church. Once again in the Johannine writings, we find teaching about the Holy Spirit as present in the world, bringing the world to a knowledge of righteousness and sin and judgement (John 16.8). In the Pauline writings, we find a recognition that the prior work of the Holy Spirit is indeed necessary for conversion itself (1 Cor. 2.14–16; 12.3; 2 Cor. 3.4—4.6; Eph. 1.17–20; 3.14–19).[3] In other words, if the Holy Spirit were not working in the world, not working among men and women everywhere of all cultures, of all kinds, the recognition of the truth of the gospel would not at all be possible. So we base the possibility of dialogue with people of all kinds on these principles, which we believe have been derived from the Bible.

—— The Witness of the Bible ——

More generally, we need urgently, I believe, to recognize that the Bible is a complex collection of documents written in a variety of situations and contexts and cultures, and that, although there is an underlying unity about the Bible, there is also a great variety in the Bible's responses to many matters, including the question of people of other faiths.[4] Let us explore some of these approaches. There is first of all an approach, or a response, that is wholly negative. Let us put within such an approach the ways in which the Israelites treated the Canaanite city states when they arrived in Canaan. (I won't at this time examine whether they arrived by conquest or infiltration; perhaps it was a bit of both.) At any rate when they arrived their commitment to a theocratic egalitarianism made them destroy these city states. Those who are working in the sociology of the Old Testament see the egalitarianism of early Israel as a leading characteristic of this emerging people at the time.[5] The Canaanite city states were very hierarchical, and so one can see why Israel responded in this negative way. Then you have Elijah and the prophets of Baal: once again a negative response. Later, after the exile, you have the ways in which Ezra and Nehemiah dealt with people who wanted to co-operate with the returning exiles in the rebuilding of the temple. In both these responses, both negative, there was a fear of syncretism, a fear that the pure worship of God would somehow be mingled with beliefs that were not consonant with God's revelation as it had been given to the Jews.

Against these we have to put some positive approaches, responses and events. Take the response to the Canaanite city states, for example. On the one hand there was the rejection of hierarchy, on the other hand there was a gradual assimilation of the religious symbols of the Canaanites. If you read a description of the building of the temple of Solomon this becomes clear, and the temple itself, as replacing the ark of the tabernacle as a focus for Israelite worship, indicated a shift from being desert nomads to being a settled people (1 Kings 7—9). But think also of Melchizedek encountering Abraham. We have to recognize that the story, as it comes to us, has been edited in different ways at different times in the history of Israel. It is not that there has been no reflection on the story; within the development of Israel itself there has been, and yet what we have clearly is a Canaanite priest king, the very thing that the early Israelites were concerned to reject, bringing bread and wine to Abraham the patriarch of all the faithful, and Abraham making an offering to Melchizedek! (Gen. 14.18–20). Now who was Melchizedek? There is later reflection on him, as I say, not only in the book of Genesis but in the Psalms, 'thou art a priest forever according to the order of Melchizedek' (Ps. 110–4). It is clear that such an order was not Aaronic. What kind of order of priesthood was Melchizedek's? In the Christian tradition, of course, Melchizedek has been seen as a type of Christ himself and the priesthood of Christ, in the Letter to the Hebrews, for example, has been related to the priesthood of Melchizedek (Heb. 7). There is a positive encounter with great potential for reflection by the people of God! Then there are others: there is Balaam, for example, and the fact that he was called to prophesy *for* Israel, on behalf of Israel, in the presence of their enemies (Num. 22—24). It is true that Balaam is shown as coming to a rather sticky end later (Num. 31.8), but that cannot detract from the fact that he prophesied in an authentic way for Israel. In more political terms, there is, of course, the figure of Cyrus and the way in which he functioned as a liberator for Israel (Isa. 45.1–6). In the book of the prophet Malachi, in the first chapter, there is that famous passage where the prophet is comparing the offerings of the people of Israel to the offerings of the Gentiles, to the disadvantage as it were of the people of Israel. There is inescapably some reference here to worship, though there may also be reference to ethical behaviour because the usual words used for the wholeness of sacrifice are not used in the passage; rather, words that are more generally used in the Bible for moral behaviour are used.[6]

But perhaps the most significant aspect of the biblical witness that we need to consider is the developing realization in Israel that their God was the God of the whole world, that he was the God of every nation, of every people. Again, responses to this realization vary in the Bible from a felt calling that God's universality needed to be expressed in terms of judgement on certain peoples. I mean this is, by and large, the witness of the books of Joshua and Judges, though not wholly so. As we have seen, this is replaced then by an approach that regards Zion as the centre of devotion to God, to Yahweh, and the other peoples are seen as eventually coming to Zion to make their submission to the God of Israel. Yes, God is the God of the whole world, but if people want to respond to his universal lordship they must do so in terms of Israel, the way in which Israel has responded must also be the model for them. Later on this becomes known as the Judaizing tendency. If you want to respond to God's revelation, even in Christ, you must do so in the way the Jews have done. Of course, we all know that the early Church rejected such an interpretation but it has been a strong element in the tradition and it affects some of our contemporary attitudes in this area.

The third approach has to do with a growing realization that God, if he is the God of the whole world, of every people, must be working in the histories of those people. Now, sometimes that may be seen as judgement, but on many occasions it is seen as salvation. Sometimes that salvation is projected on to the future, in the great visions in Isaiah, for example, where Egypt and Assyria are seen to be as much, at least potentially, God's people as Israel. It is right to interpret the nineteenth chapter of Isaiah as eschatalogical, to project it into the future, but that is not always the case with other passages. Sometimes God's work among people is about the past, so that in Amos 9 God is shown to have a purpose, not only in the Exodus of the people of Israel from Egypt, but in the histories of the Ethiopians, the Syrians, the Philistines, all the neighbours that Israel had encountered. This is extremely important for our attitude to certain emphases in biblical theology. We are greatly indebted to those who have developed the paradigmatic concept of salvation history, that is to say that God's revelation is not to be understood primarily as propositions about belief, but that God's revelation is about his activity among his people and in the world. The biblical salvation history is very largely about God's action, God's revelation to the people of Israel, that culminates, comes to a climax, in the incarnation, though not of course to an end. But if this is normative salvation history, why is it normative? What is its function? It can be normative only if it leads us to a recognition, to a discernment, of other salvation histories, that is to say, and I believe this to be the teaching of the Bible, that there is a salvation history among every people, every culture. It is not easy of course to discern such a salvation history, it is very problematic, but it is possible for us to discern this salvation history, with whatever difficulty, because of the normative salvation history that we have of the people of Israel in the Bible.

I have not commented particularly on the attitude of Jesus himself, but perhaps one or two remarks are necessary. One is that liberation theologians have underlined the importance of what they call the Galilean option, that is to say the importance of the choice of Galilee by Jesus for his earthly ministry. Their point is that Galilee was *chosen*. It was not an accident that Galilee came to be the focus for his earthly ministry, this was a deliberate choice because Galilee was all that the religious and political and economic establishment was not. Jesus deliberately chose to be among people who were not powerful, who were not wealthy and who were not learned.[7] But from our point of view Galilee is important because Galilee is Galilee of the nations and it is possible to read this choice as a choice for pluralism. Galilee was among the first of the parts of the northern kingdom to be conquered by the Assyrians, depopulated through exile of its original inhabitants, and repopulated by people from different parts of the Assyrian empire.[8] So by the time of Jesus, it had a very mixed population, people of very different beliefs, and some of the encounters in the gospel are about that: 'Many will come from east and west and sit at table with Abraham and Isaac and Jacob' (Matt. 8.11). The Galilean option then is an option for pluralism against the orthodoxy of Jerusalem. Secondly, it is also where the risen Christ is present, ahead of his disciples. In the resurrection narrative in Matthew, the disciples are told to go to

Galilee, where Christ will meet them. It is possible to read this in two different ways. It is possible to say that what the risen Christ is saying is that he will *lead* the disciples into Galilee, that is to say, he will go ahead of them. The other is to read it in such a way as to say that he is *present* in Galilee ahead of them, before they get there. However you read it, the point is that when we approach people of other cultures, other communities, other language groups, we can be sure that Christ is ahead of us. Very often the unspoken, implicit assumption in a lot of mission work is that of taking Christ to people, and that expression is sometimes used. Now I know what people are saying and it is not wholly incorrect to speak like that, but we have to be on our guard lest we become, or think that we are, more than in fact we are. Christ is already ahead of us in Galilee.

What then is dialogue in the rest of the New Testament and in the early history of the Christian Church? The words that are used in the New Testament are *dialegomai* and *dialogizomai*. Both mean something like an argument for the sake of persuasion. This is the way in which the word is used in relation to the activity of the apostle Paul in the Acts of the Apostles (Acts 17.2; 18.4 etc.). This is also the sense in which the word is used in Justin, for example, in his dialogue with Trypho the Jew, a dialogue conducted so that the interlocutor may be convinced of the truth of the gospel. Indeed, we find this meaning still in use at the later end of the patristic period, by John of Damascus. Now John of Damascus is a very interesting figure because he came from a family which had opened the doors of Damascus to the Muslim armies. A Christian family, they had done this to get away from the oppression of Christian Byzantium. I think this is, if anything, a matter for profound repentance for Christians. Not only did he come from such a family, but for a while he held very important office under the Ummayad Caliphs. Apart from his great theological work which is the basis for a great deal of the theological method that we still use, he wrote two dialogues, or accounts of dialogues, with Muslims.[9] Now again the word as it is used by John means arguing with somebody, conversing with somebody, with a view to persuading them of the truth of the gospel.

This sense, this meaning of the word dialogue, comes right down to modern times in the way in which Hume uses the word, for example. His *Dialogues Concerning Natural Religion* are about convincing people of certain things that he believed to be true.[10] Nevertheless, in the patristic and perhaps the New Testament sense of the word, there is in the background something about the *dialectical method* that was used by the ancients a great deal to arrive at truth. Think of Plato's accounts of the dialogues of Socrates: conversations which result in a perception of truth that dogmatic teaching does not. The question-and-answer method results in genuine discovery of something new. Now this is very important for dialogue as it is today. While Christians will want to present truth as they see it revealed in Jesus Christ and in the Gospels, there is always a sense in which dialogue with people produces a new kind of appreciation of some aspect of truth, even Christian truth. For me, and this is a personal testimony, my dialogue with Muslims over the years has resulted in a fresh appreciation of the doctrine of the unity of God which in some cases is seriously compromised by certain kinds of Christian trinitarian theology. It is very interesting to me to see how the Western Christian theological tradition, which in the past used to emphasize the unity of God over against the diversity of the persons, has in this century gone completely over to a version of Eastern Christian thinking without the safeguards of classical Eastern Christian thinking. Now that perhaps is another matter, but just to alert you to the fact that dialogue can result in something new when it is conducted in this way.

—— The Practice of Dialogue ——

How is dialogue practised? We have seen that Professor Eric Sharpe, now in Australia, has distinguished four different ways in which dialogue is conducted today. The first he calls discursive dialogue, that is to say when partners come together and exchange information about each other's beliefs. This is a necessary aspect of dialogue. From the Christian point of view it is an aspect of dialogue where Christians must be very attentive to their partners, talk less and listen more; of course, we are not known for this in the world, but when people are telling us what they believe we need to listen very attentively. Then Sharpe talks about dialogue which has to do with a common recognition of our humanity. Again this is a crucial area for dialogue today as we seek to discover each other's commitment to, for example, human rights and the rights of women. In the context of dialogue with Muslims, this is an area that bristles with difficulties. Both sides talk about human rights, but when Christians and Muslims talk about human rights together they soon discover that their perceptions are very different. What are Christian perceptions about Qur'ānic penal law, for example, and what are Muslim perceptions? This is a matter for dialogue, and it is something that is not easily resolved. Third, Eric Sharpe refers to dialogue that is for the building up of community: if we are citizens of a particular nation, if we are members of a particular community, we will all be committed to the building up of that community. Dialogue is very important to ensure that we are working together for the building up of one community and not engaged in activities that divide communities into Muslim and Christian sectors, Hindu and Muslim and Christian sectors and so on. Finally, Sharpe talks about the sort of dialogue which is about the sharing of spiritual experience. Once again to give an example from Muslim/Christian history, there has been for thirteen hundred years dialogue between Christians in the mystical ascetical tradition and Muslims in the mystical ascetical tradition. Sufism, as a phenomenon in the world of Islam, is glad in many respects to refer to encounters with Christians that have enriched the Sufi traditon. From the Christian point of view, a great deal of mystical terminology that is used by Christians in the Muslim world comes from the Sufi tradition. So this dialogue about the exchange of spiritual experience is important.[11]

The Vatican has recently issued a document which also attempts to classify kinds of dialogue, and once again it seems very like the division that Sharpe made all those years ago. The Vatican's divisions are the dialogue of life, the dialogue of deeds, the dialogue of specialists and the dialogue of the interior life. So you can see how they correspond with Sharpe's division.[12] People, sometimes, do not give enough value to the dialogue of specialists. In some cases this *has* been sterile. where it has been overly concerned with classical issues and there has been a danger in some respects of a merely antiquarian interest. But one way forward which is proving to be quite fruitful is a model which has been taken from intra-Christian ecumenical dialogue. That is a model of dialogue where a group of scholars from each side come together for a considerable period of time, say five or six years, correspond with each other, meet each other regularly, and consider one theme such as the Scriptures in Islam and Christianity – so that they may come to a common mind about the place of Scripture in religion, for example. There has been a fruitful dialogue between French-speaking Muslims and French-speaking Christians in this particular area which has been very revealing about how far the Muslims are prepared to go in their understanding not only of their own Scripture but of the Bible.[13]

—— *Dialogue and Mission* ——

The Church Missionary Society has been committed for many scores of years to the view that dialogue is the presupposition for Christian mission, for Christian witness. In other words, there can be no authentic Christian witness without prior dialogue. Unless we understand people's beliefs, their culture, the idiom of that culture, their thought forms, the intellectual tradition, the artistic tradition, the faith tradition, unless we understand these we will not be able to witness to people authentically as Christians. This is behind the strongly incarnational approach that CMS has taken in the past, and continues to take today. Mission is not hit and run. People these days are talking about 'non-resident missionaries'. In some cases these are necessary, of course. But that will never be, I hope, a model for CMS, because mission must be incarnational, and this is why so many distinguished missionaries – Temple Gairdner in Egypt, W. D. P. Hill in India, in our own days people like Roger Hooker and Christopher Lamb – spent years in incarnational situations learning about cultures and languages and peoples before they felt able to witness to them of Christian faith and Christian truth. This is absolutely essential. So mission cannot be hit and run. It cannot be at a distance. A great deal of time and effort is being expended in the world today in preaching the gospel to people through the mass media. Now in some ways this is necessary, as some parts of the world cannot be reached in any other way. Think of the way in which the Bible was broadcast at dictation speed to the people of Albania. But again it can never be an ideal way, because of the commitment to incarnation and to dialogue as the presupposition for witness.

But dialogue is not only preparatory to witness, *it is also the means to witness*, and here I have been somewhat distressed by the ambivalence in the ecumenical movement on this question. Some documents, such as the guidelines on dialogue produced by the British Council of Churches, say clearly that dialogue is a medium for authentic witness.[14] But other documents of the World Council deny this and make every effort to claim that the occasion of dialogue must not be an occasion for Christian witness.[15] I think the concern behind this is that our partners should not see our efforts at dialogue as efforts at proselytization, and that concern is valid. On the other hand, I cannot see dialogue in its fullness without the opportunity for both sides to witness to their faith in trust that the partners recognize each other's integrity. For Christians, dialogue will always be about listening and learning; our partner's faith may shed unexpected light on our own. We must, however, also be committed to let the light of Christ shine through our conversation and reflection. Without that, dialogue remains unfulfilled for the Christian.

— 8 —

Islam in the Modern World:
Some Questions

✳

Muslims are often heard today to be saying that Islam is a universal faith aspiring to include, if not actually including, people of all races and nationalities. Because of such an understanding, Muslims, naturally, resist attempts to describe them in merely ethnic categories, especially in situations where they are a clearly identifiable minority. Christians should applaud such a desire to be understood primarily in terms of one's faith, but both Muslims and Christians will need to recognize that this makes the theological questions which arise from encounters between Muslims and people of other faiths, especially Christians, of paramount importance.

—— Diversity in Islam ——

Like Christianity, Islam has a rich and varied theological tradition. This is seen not only in the careful and detailed exegesis of the Qur'ān by the commentators or in the careful gathering of traditions about the Prophet of Islam, but also in the free-ranging speculation of those influenced by Hellenistic Neoplatonism and in the devotional reflections of those who had a powerful, mystical experience of God, as among the Sufis. Even those who criticized the unorthodoxy of the philosophers often used philosophical categories to do so, as in Ghazzali's *Tahafut Al-Falasifa* (or Refutation of the Philosophers)[1]. Similarly, those critical of the excesses of the monistic, *wahdat Al-wujud*, school of Sufism, such as Sheikh Sarhandi and Shah Waliullah, continued, nevertheless, to stand within the broad, Sufi world-view.[2]

It is clear that such a tradition has developed in response to a variety of situations in which Muslims have found themselves and to which they have tried to relate their faith. The emergence of *Kalam*, or formal theology, for instance, takes place in a Greek philosophical milieu often mediated through oriental Christian translators.[3] In the same way, the rise of Sufism, while deeply rooted in the Qur'ān and the piety of the

84

early Muslims, is explicitly acknowledged as having been influenced by the example of the Christian monks of Egypt and Syria.[4] Perhaps the best example is the way in which *Fiqh*, or Islamic Law, was codified in the early days. It has been shown that the early jurists were sensitive to their contexts and took into account not only the customs and traditions of their times but also the preceding legal tradition (such as Roman Law). The place of *ʿada*, or custom, is recognized by law in many Islamic societies and has for long allowed jurists to make a distinction between the religious law (*Shariʿah*) of the *ummah* (the Muslim community) and the civil law of the state.[5]

—— *Coping with Change* ——

As with other faiths, Islam in the modern world is facing a situation in which the rate of change is accelerating. Each faith has to seek the resources to meet contemporary challenges in its own origins, its own history and its own traditions. Those, both within and outside Islam, who urge a constructive engagement with modernity are often accused of promoting a 'compromise' with secularity or liberalism. This need not, however, be the case at all. Such an engagement can take place on Islamic terms by using the resources available within Islam itself.[6] It is true, of course, that those who are not Muslims are often very interested in how Islam deals with contemporary issues. Religious minorities in the Islamic world are interested because their future may depend on the kinds of responses that are made. Citizens of countries where Muslims are a minority are interested because many of them want to live in peace and harmony with their Muslim neighbours.

It is possible, of course, for the challenge of modernity to be met by retreating into obscurantism. Nor is this a possibility for Muslims alone. Believers in different faith-traditions have, from time to time, sought refuge from the perplexities of the world in exactly this way. The nostalgia for a golden age of certainties has sometimes led to the emergence of a full-blown fundamentalism. Once again, this is not limited to the world of Islam but *has* been especially characteristic of it in recent times. It is true that there has been a recrudescence of various forms of chauvinistic nationalism in different parts of the world and that religion is sometimes an element in this. Much of Hindu revivalism in India today is of this kind. If, however, fundamentalism is described as a literal understanding of the primary documents of a faith and a desire to apply their moral, cultural and legal demands in their entirety without sufficient attention to the contexts in which believers have to live, then Christianity and Islam emerge as the two faiths which are experiencing fundamentalism in a significant way at this time. In the case of Christianity, fundamentalism is often limited to the way in which the Bible is understood, and the consequences of this for piety and for personal and social ethics. It is comparatively rarely that movements like 'moral majority' and R. J. Rushdoony's 'reconstructionism' produce comprehensive ideologies which include matters of state and of law as well as attitudes to piety and morality.[7]

In Islam, however, in recent years, there have emerged movements which have had comprehensive, and even coercive, ideologies from both politically conservative and revolutionary points of view. As far as their comprehensiveness is concerned, they can be compared only to Marxism-Leninism in terms of recent history. Islam is seen not only as influencing every area of life (other faiths too claim to do this), but detailed legislation is provided for every aspect of personal and social life. This, naturally results in the restriction of choice and the loss of flexibility. The reasons for the emergence of these movements are many and complex, but they include a reaction to the experience of colonialism, the failure of both capitalism and socialism to bring about prosperous and just societies in the Muslim world, and the search for an authentic Islamic identity. In countries where Muslims are a minority, they have often experienced marginalization and even discrimination. This has had the effect of 'radicalizing' the politics of these communities, and particularly of the young among them, in a fundamentalist direction. Fundamentalist movements have provided a basis for identity and belonging for many young people who have lost confidence in the society in which they live. Fundamentalism offers them community, hope, and the possibility of a struggle to bring about change. It also, of course, 'ghettoizes' them and makes it more difficult for them to make sense of the wider society in which they are placed.

—— Development and Change ——

But what other responses may there be to the challenge of modernity? In the end, it is for Muslims to answer this question, and many are engaged in doing so. Christians who see themselves as friends of Muslims and sympathetic observers of Islam can only point to the kinds of issues which need consideration. There is, for instance, the need for greater *consciousness* of the width of Islamic tradition – a tradition which has emerged from the encounter of Islam with a great variety of cultures, world-views, and values. The tradition itself has many aspects to it, such as the legal, the theological, and the mystical. Each of these, in turn, has within itself particular responses to specific situations. Awareness of the great diversity within the tradition will allow for greater flexibility in responding to contemporary issues.

Secondly, an intellectual culture needs to be encouraged which will be *critical* in its approach to the sources of the faith. This will certainly involve an *historical* awareness of the particular circumstances in which Islam took its rise, its relations with Judaism and Christianity, and the historical elements within the Qur'ān itself. This should lead also to an interest in the *literary* background to the Qur'ān, its form and sources, and its relation to the Judaeo-Christian Scriptures and other literature. Within Islam, *Kalam* theology offers a way of relating the eternal Word of God to the historical circumstances in which the Word is revealed. This should make it possible to engage in a literary-historical study of the text of the Qur'ān without compromising the divine revelation which it is seen to mediate. From time to time, Western orientalists have engaged in such study and, more recently, Muslim scholars such as Ameer Ali Syed, Muhammad Iqbal and Fazlur Rahman have also adopted this approach. There has always been a critical study of the transmission of the *Ahadith* or the traditions of the Prophet. Commentaries have also been written to explain their meaning to subsequent generations. Is there a need for a more rigorous examination of the *contents* of the various authorized collections, so that, by comparison with each other and with the Qur'ān itself, their authenticity might be established? This is extremely important as some traditions, at least, are at the basis of provisions in the *Sharicah*. From the time of Shah Waliullah, traditionists have distinguished between the eternal principles of prophetic teaching and the *particular* ways in which they are implemented in the culture to which the prophet has been sent. The former are valid for all ages and all times but the latter cannot be imposed indiscriminately on other ages and cultures.[8] This vision is of very great relevance today.

—— *Development and Its Basis in Tradition* ——

There has to be encouragement for a greater responsiveness to *change*. This does *not* mean that the tradition itself has to be changing constantly, nor should it involve cheap compromises with the 'spirit of the age'. Rather, resources have to be developed within the tradition itself, so that believers can engage with contemporary life from the perspective of their faith. ʿAllama Iqbal has referred to 'the principle of movement' in the structure of Islam. It is extremely important to discern what the elements of this are and how they can be used to engage with the contemporary world. The possibility of exercising *ijtihad* has existed from the time of the Prophet of Islam. *Ijtihad* may be understood as rigorous reflection on the sources of Islamic law with a view to forming an independent judgement rather than placing one's entire reliance on precedent alone. In particular schools of law, the application of *qiyas*, or analogical reasoning in relation to the primary sources of law, may be extended or limited (a procedure known as *naskh*), if the jurist feels that this is necessary. In the *Hanafi* school, jurists were allowed a certain amount of freedom in determining which procedures were suitable in the light of the actual situation (this is known as *istihsan* – or holding for better). Similarly, the *Malikis* had what is known as *istislah*: the right of a jurist to set aside a judgement based on *qiyas* for the sake of the greater good of the community. Even the more conservative *Shafiʿi* school had the principle of *istishab*. According to them, a law remains the same for a given situation as long as it is not certain that the situation has, in fact, altered. This is clearly a more conservative position, compared to the other two, but does, nevertheless, leave some room for movement.[9] Movements of revival, moreover, such as that of Ibn Taimiyya or Ibn Tumart, from which today's fundamentalists often seek inspiration, began with a rejection of the existing *ijmaʿ* or consensus so that they could proceed afresh from the primary sources.

Traditionally, *ijmaʿ* has been limited to a particular time, place or group of people. (e.g., the city of Medina, the companions of the Prophet etc.). Conceptually, however, it has to do with the mind of the whole *ummah* as to what are the expressions of authentic Islam. From the time of the disappearance of the Ottoman Caliphate, Muslims in various countries have been discussing how the *ijmaʿ* can be articulated. It has often been suggested, for example, that the legislative assemblies of the various Muslim countries should have a part to play in the articulation of *ijmaʿ*, at least in matters which relate to their particular situation. In this they may seek the guidance of *ʿulema* (divines), but the latter are to be seen mainly as advisers rather than as those who determine what the *ijmaʿ* is in any specific matter. Many Muslim countries and jurists have seen for some time now that the traditional codifications need to be reformed in the light of modern conditions. Muhammad ʿAbduh, for instance, who became Grand Mufti in Egypt at the turn of the century, used the Maliki principle of *istislah* to argue for reform.

He believed that traditional codifications should be replaced by new laws which were capable of development and which would not themselves solidify into rigid codes. Flexibility was the great need of the age, and in the formulation of new laws the general good of society should be kept to the fore. Many of his *fatwas* (or judicial pronounce-ments) greatly eased relations between Muslims and the *Ahl Al-Kitab* (People of the Book i.e., mainly Jews and Christians). He also made a distinction between *riba* (or usury), which is forbidden, and interest charged by banks and other financial institutions. Like others, such as the translator of the Qur'ān, Yusuf ᶜAli, he accepted that the latter was necessary for modern commerce.[10]

ᶜAbduh's example can be paralleled in other contexts such as that of Turkey or the South Asian subcontinent. Individuals like Zia in Turkey and Sir Syed Ahmad Khan in India also argued for radical reform in the Islamic legal system. More significant, perhaps, are the reforms which Muslim governments began to make from about the middle of the nineteenth century. Within the Ottoman Empire, the status of *dhimmis* (protected religious minorities) began to change markedly as a result of the Edict of Gulhaneh and subsequent measures. Theocratic views of the state began gradually to be replaced by nationalisms of various kinds and it became more possible for religious minorities to play an active role in the affairs of state. The role of Arab Christians, for example, in the emergence of Arab nationalism is well documented.[11] In the areas of commercial and penal law there seems to have been much borrowing from Western sources. When the civil law was codified, however, an attempt was made to draw on the work of a wide range of Sunni scholars. The well-known British Islamicist, Sir Norman Anderson, has referred to this process of compiling law from a wide range of sources as *talfiq* (a term used, elsewhere, for making patchwork quilts etc!). The main criterion for choosing particular opinions seems to have been their suitability for contemporary circumstances. In time, a consensus emerged that the law in Muslim countries should indeed be based on principles derived from the *Shariᶜah* but that, within this framework, there may be adaptation and borrowing to meet the needs of the times.

Family law has often proved to be most resistant to reform. Even here, however, the right of a wife to seek a judicial divorce was recognized as early as 1915. This recognition is based on the well-established principle of *khulaᶜ* found in certain Sunni schools. Countries such as Tunisia, Syria and Pakistan have introduced codified forms of family law which have the the effect of restricting polygamy, recognizing the right of wives to seek a judicial divorce in certain circumstances and introducing a minimum age for marriage. Attempts are also being made to check abuses of the *mehr* system which is meant to provide maintenance for the wife in the event of divorce, and some groups are even campaigning to have the *mehr* arrangements at the wedding made in such a way that the wife receives *regular maintenance*, not simply a one-off payment, if there is a divorce.

As far as penal law is concerned, reformers such as Waliullah, Syed Ahmad Khan, Ameer Ali and ᶜAbduh have argued that, while the *principles* of Islamic jurisprudence, such as honesty and fair dealing in society and fidelity in married life, need always to be promoted, they need not be promoted in ways identical with those of nomadic society in the seventh century CE! Each age and culture has to determine how Islamic values are to be promoted and law and order maintained in the light of its own circumstances and of advances in knowledge, technology and social structures. There cannot be blind imitation (*taqlid*) of the past.

There is, similarly, a long tradition of thought where fresh considerations of the notion of *jihad* (or holy war) arise out of and are applied to specific circumstances. In the case of those non-Muslim countries, for instance, where Muslims live as a minority and where their rights and freedoms are protected, there cannot be *jihad* to subdue such countries to Islamic rule. Many Muslims thinkers, including Iqbal, limit *jihad* to self-defence.[12] Others, such as Ubaidullah Sindhi, think of it primarily in terms of social revolution; a struggle for justice in society.[13] The Sufis, on the other hand, see *jihad* particularly as a struggle against the evil inclinations of one's own self. Yusuf ᶜAli, the well-known translator of the Qur'ān, thinks of *jihad* in terms of self-sacrifice. For him, it is essentially earnest and ceaseless activity in the service of God.[14]

All of these different ways of understanding *jihad* are important if, on the one hand, Muslims are to be equipped to defend the legitimate interests of their community and, on the other, to resist those who would reduce the notion to what YusufᶜAli has called 'mere brutal fighting'. Just as Christians need to refine the idea of the just war in the light of contemporary conditions, so Muslims need to develop a coherent view of *jihad* based on the different aspects of their own tradition.

—— *Muslims as a Minority* ——

In situations where Muslims are a socially and politically significant minority, social, political, and legal traditions need to develop in ways which recognize the presence of Muslims and their sentiments and aspirations. This may be seen, for example, in the way in which the Law provides a basis for respect of people's beliefs and prevents slanderous or libellous attacks on them while, at the same time, preserving freedom of expression, genuine enquiry and criticism. It may also be seen in how such contexts are able to accommodate Muslim views on social behaviour, education and religious practices. In many areas, including dress, diet, and devotion, Muslims can follow their own customs without in any way coming into conflict with the legal traditions and even customs of the majority. It is often prejudice, rather than law or genuine custom, which prevents them from doing so. There *are* areas, however, where the legal situation has to be considered. In Britain, for instance, the possibility of discrimination on religious grounds, where employment is concerned, needs to be addressed.

In such situations, however, Muslims too will need to exercise rigorous *ijtihad* so that the demands of the *Shariʿah* are related to their particular circumstances as minorities in rapidly changing societies. They will also need to distinguish more and more between mere custom and what their faith really requires of them in a given situation. Needless to say, Muslims are not alone in facing such dilemmas. People of many faiths are having to face them in today's world. Christians, in particular, will see affinities here with the ways in which *they* have to deal with modernity and post-modernity.

In a highly mobile world, where people of different cultures and faiths are living 'cheek by jowl' with each other, it is extremely important that the proper freedoms of communities and individuals should be safeguarded. Christians, where they have influence, should ensure that people of other faiths have the freedom to worship and to practise and propagate their faith freely. They should struggle for the elimination of all discrimination based, among other things, on religion. Muslims too need to rediscover resources within Islam itself which allow others the freedoms Muslims, rightly, want for themselves. There is, after all, 'no compulsion in matters of faith' (Qur'ān 2.256) and even the Prophet of Islam was told not to *compel* people to believe in his message (Q 10.99, 88.21–26).

The *principle of reciprocity* is often being talked about these days. It should not, however, be reduced to the stance that Christians will struggle for the rights of Muslims only when Christian minorities in Muslim lands have similar rights. Nor should Muslims make rights for Christians dependent on how *they* are treated in situations where they are a minority. Rather, each side should be committed to basic rights and freedoms for all in every place. People of different faiths should have the freedom to practise and to propagate their faith in every situation. Muslims and Christians should commit themselves to seeing that this happens in societies where they have influence. In this way they will promote peace and harmony not only in their own societies but well beyond.

— 9 —

Prayer and Spirituality
in Muslim Thought

✳

—— Prophetic Consciousness ——

Those chapters of the Qur'ān which are regarded as chronologically
early (though not necessarily appearing early in the present order of
the Qur'ān) are mostly the ones which are brief and are either
invocatory or 'prophetic' in content. They tend to be permeated with a
sense of the numinous, which brings awe in its wake and which makes
demands of a moral nature on human beings. The spirituality of these
chapters may rightly be called a spirituality of the 'prophetic' type. The
most well-known example of these chapters is the one called *Fātiḥa*
(the word means 'opening' and, indeed, this chapter is found at the
very beginning of the Qur'ān). The *Fātiḥa* is a short prayer which first
praises God the Creator of the universe and the Judge of all and then
calls on him for guidance along the right path. Its role in Muslim
devotion has often been compared to that of the Lord's Prayer in
Christian devotion.[1] Louis Massignon, a well known Christian scholar
of Islam, called it 'a prayer of the community of Abraham'.[2] The
'prophetic' type of spirituality is not, of course, limited to these
chapters of the Qur'ān. It may be said, however, that these chapters
typify such spirituality. In these chapters an experience of God as
'other', as utterly transcendent, is often portrayed. Experience of God,
moreover, is not for its own sake but to guide human beings to right
action. An Indian Muslim mystic, ᶜAbdul Quddūs Gangōhī, is reputed
to have said, '*Muḥammad* of Arabia ascended to the highest heaven and
returned. I swear by Almighty God that if I had reached such a state, I
would never have returned!' Muhammad Iqbal, a great Muslim scholar
of this century, remarks that this sums up the difference between
'prophetic' and 'mystic' consciousness. The mystic is concerned to
preserve and to cultivate 'the repose of unitary experience', whereas
the 'prophet' is concerned with translating an experience of the divine
into action which tends to change the world.[3]

Mystic Consciousness

Apart from this 'prophetic' consciousness, there is also in the Qur'ān a sense of God's pervasiveness in the world and his nearness to human beings. The famous 'Light verse' in the Qur'ān is regarded by many Muslims as illustrative of God's all-pervading glory:

> God is the Light of the heavens and the earth.
> The parable of his Light is as if there were a Niche
> And within it a Lamp;
> The Lamp enclosed in Glass:
> The Glass as it were
> A brilliant star:
> Lit from a blessed Tree,
> An olive, neither of the East
> Nor of the West,
> whose oil is well-nigh Luminous.
> Though fire scarce touched it:
> Light upon Light!
> God doth guide
> whom he will
> To his Light (24.35).

God is also spoken of as nearer to human beings than their jugular veins (50.16), though it may be that here it is his omniscience which is being emphasized rather than his immanence. In 5:57, it is said that God will bring forth a people whom he will love and who will love him. Close fellowship with God is thus declared as at least possible in the Qur'ān. The closest encounter that a human being has had with God, for Muslim tradition, remains that of the prophet of Islam's vision which is recorded in chapter 53 of the Qur'ān.

The origins of mystical consciousness in Islam are to be found in such a sense of God's pervasiveness and nearness. It is true though that the Muslim mystical tradition developed in relation to the living and ever-present reality of Christian monasticism. Admiration for the spirituality of Christian religious is already present in the Qur'ān itself (5:85) and is acknowledged by both Christian and Muslim scholars as a source of inspiration for the early Muslim mystics.[4] Nor is a Muslim appreciation of Christian spirituality totally a thing of the past. Some contemporary Muslim scholars give it an important place in their own work today.[5] It is also true that other influences on Islam, such as Neo-platonism and Indian monism, have made a formative impact on Sufism (Islamic mysticism). In the early period, Muslim mystical tradition was usually theistic and emphasized personal devotion to God. As influences other than Christianity became more important, however, the tradition became preoccupied with themes such as the unity of all being (*waḥdat al-wujūd*), the absorption and annihilation of the individual self in the life of God and even the necessity for an inner kind of knowledge (*maʿrifa*). Despite the many and diverse influences on the formation of the mystical tradition in Islam, Muslims have continued to seek authentication of their spiritual experience in the Qurʾān and in the practice of their prophet, the *Sunnah*.

—— Ritual Prayer and Meditation ——

The *Ṣalāt* is the ritual prayer which is obligatory for a Muslim. It has to be said five times a day and consists mostly of recitation from the Qurʾān and the adoption of certain postures, such as prostration, bowing, etc., which are suggestive of worship. Perhaps it can be said that the Muslim experience of God as utterly transcendent and beyond human comprehension is focused and defined in the *Ṣalāt*. The opening prayer, for example, which is said before the recitation of the *Fātiḥa*, goes like this: 'I have turned my face towards him who created the heavens and the earth, true in faith, a Muslim and I am not one of the idolators'. Sometimes, after the recitation of the *Fātiḥa*, other verses such as the famous throne verse are recited:

> God! there is no god but he,
> The Living.
> The Self-subsisting, Eternal.
> No slumber can seize him,
> Nor sleep. His are all things
> in the heavens and on earth.
> Who is there can intercede
> in his presence except
> as he permits? He knows
> what is Present and Past.
> They know nothing of his knowledge,
> except in so far as he wishes.
> His throne embraces the heavens and the earth.
> He feels no fatigue in guarding and preserving them,
> He is the exalted, the mighty (2.255).

In prostration, the worshipper says, 'Glory be to my Lord, the most exalted and to him praise!' The institution of the *Ṣalāt* (the word itself is of Aramaic origin) seems to be modelled, in its recitation and posture, on Christian and Jewish worship, particularly on the monastic offices of the Christian church.

The *Duʿa* (or invocatory prayer), which is sometimes said in conjunction with the *Ṣalāt* but which can be offered at other times as well, is perhaps a context in which nearness to God is experienced by the Muslim. Constance Padwick quotes from a *Duʿa* of a famous Muslim saint, ʿAbdul Qādir Al-Jīlānī. 'O God we take refuge with thy friendship from thy aversion, with thy nearness from thy distance, and we take refuge with thee from thee.'[6] Already in the Qur'ān (e.g. *Sūrah* 97), the night is the time when God's message is revealed, and in Muslim tradition it has become the time when God's nearness is especially experienced. Prophetic tradition speaks of God coming down at night to hear the petitions of the believers and a special non-obligatory form of *Ṣalāt* called *tahajjud* can be performed in the middle of the night. A well-known Muslim prayer speaks thus of divine intimacy with 'lovers of God', at this time of the night:

> My God and my Lord, eyes are at rest, stars are setting, hushed are the movements of birds in their nests, of monsters in the deep. And thou art the Just who knowest no change, the Equity that severeth not, the Everlasting that passeth not away. The doors of kings are locked, watched by their bodyguards, but thy door is open to him who calls on thee. My Lord, each lover is now alone with his beloved, and thou art for me the Beloved.[7]

The similarities between the practices of Christian Syrian and Egyptian ascetics and Muhammad's meditations during the night in the cave of *Ḥirā* have often been noticed. As Islam moved into the 'christianized' culture of West Asia and Africa, traditions about night vigils began to be emphasized and keeping vigil became an important part not only of Muslim ascetical practice but of popular devotion too.[8]

—— Dhikr and the Jesus Prayer ——

One aspect of Muslim devotional practice which has to be noticed is that of *dhikr*. The term itself means 'remembrance' and is related to Hebrew and Aramaic words for 'mentioning the name of the Lord' (e.g. Ps. 20.7). In the Qur'ān it sometimes has this meaning and is specifically related to the performance of the *Ṣalāt* (87.15; 33.41; 4.142; 5.91; 62.9). At other times, it seems to mean the remembrance of God during the pilgrimage (2.200) or in the context of covenant (2.152). In Muslim devotion, however, the term has come to mean the recitation of certain fixed formulae (usually based on the attributes of

God). *Dhikr* can be solidary or solitary. As communal exercises, gatherings for the purpose of *dhikr* have great appeal for the masses. At such gatherings, the rhythms of sound and movement create a trance-like state among the devotees so that the daily pressures of life are forgotten and ordinary inhibitions overcome. *Dhikr* can be performed on one's own too. Indeed, some Sufis (Muslim mystics) claim that there is never a time when the devotee is free of the obligation to perform *dhikr*.[9]

The outward recitation of the formula, accompanied by suitable movements of the body, is said to induce a state of interior recollection and concentration. Bishop Timothy Ware has pointed out that the practice of reciting the Jesus Prayer was already current in Eastern Christianity from the fifth century onwards. This practice too, by means of recitation and movement, is said to assist concentration in meditation. Bishop Ware, himself, has noted the similarities between the Jesus Prayer and *dhikr*.[10] Given the close contact that existed between Christian ascetics and Muslim Sufis in the early years of Islam, these similarities are remarkable indeed. The recitation of *dhikr*, meditation and ascetical practices are some of the ways in which a mystically inclined Muslim prepares for mystical experiences. There are different stages of such preparation and they are called *maqāmāt* (sing. *maqām*). They must be distinguished from the experience itself, which too can come in a variety of ways which are called *Aḥwāl* (sing. *ḥāl*). The preparation is what the human being does in order to prepare for the experience. The experience, however, is regarded as 'given' and not at all the product of human effort. Many of the *Aḥwāl* were experienced as 'union' with all things or with the Absolute itself. This experience was often explained in monistic terms drawn from Neoplatonism or the Indian monistic tradition of *Vedanta*.

—— *Kinds of Mystical Experience* ——

Many Sufis were, however, already aware that such an experience of 'union' is not the ultimate in mystical experience but only a beginning. Sheikh Aḥmad Sarhindī, the seventeenth-century Indian mystic, developed a system which went beyond the experience of monism to a fully fledged theistic experience.[11] In modern times Professor R. C. Zaehner, basing himself upon the work of Al-Qushayrī, has suggested that mystical experience is analysable in terms of the manic-depressive syndrome. In the 'manic' phase the mystic experiences a sense of identity with the rest of the universe. This is sometimes expressed in the language of nature mysticism and at other times in the language of monism. The self is spoken of as 'absorbed into' God, the Absolute or the Unity of Being. The 'depressive' phase is characterized by withdrawal from the world and a sense of 'aloneness'. The divinity of the self may be emphasized but not its unity with all being. In Indian tradition, *Samkhya* is a mystical-philosophical system which emphasizes the increasing isolation of the self on the path to perfect liberation. Extremely ascetic and eremitical tendencies within Christianity and Islam also, however, illustrate the 'depressive' phase.[12] It will be noticed that for Sarhindī, the experience of Union is but a stage on the mystical journey which, if continued, goes on to an experience of God as personal and the human self as enduring. For Zaehner, on the other hand, different experiences represent different kinds of mysticism, with theistic mysticism being neither unitive nor isolationist but relational.[13]

Similarities and Differences
Between Christian and Muslim Spiritualities

Traditionally, Christian and Muslim spirituality, even where there has been a long experience of living together and of close interaction, have developed along separate lines. For some, this is inevitable, given the very different beliefs of the two faiths. Christian spirituality is often based on the doctrine of the incarnation and its corollary, *theōsis*. Devotion is focused on God-made-human, and its ultimate goal is the divinization of the human (2 Pet. 1.3,4). These are precisely the areas of Christian belief which are rejected by the Qur'ān. Islam denies even the possibility of incarnation, basing itself on God's utter transcendence and aweful majesty (Q 5.75–80, 119f.; 9.30). Divinization, of course, would be *shirk*, associating partners with God, arguably the greatest sin in Islam! The doctrine of the incarnation leads at least some Christians to sacramental forms of devotion. Iconography, the drama of the liturgy, reaching its climax in the partaking of a sacred meal and even the use of music are justified by an appeal to the 'incarnational' or sacramental principle. God has revealed himself in the material order and the material may be regarded as a proper medium for the worship of God. In orthodox Islam at least, apart from the postures of the human body, this emphasis is missing. It is true, of course, that popular devotion has not been able to do without the sacramental and 'incarnational', and so Muslim theologies of 'incarnation' have developed hand in hand with 'sacramental' devotional practices such as the veneration of the tombs of Sufi saints and the whole *cultus* associated with them.[14] Interaction with other religious traditions can often be discerned in such developments. We have seen, however, that much of Muslim devotional practice is closely related to forms of Christian ascetical practice, and that even important ritual practices like the *Ṣalāt* have points of contact with Christian worship.

In architecture too there is a close relationship. When Islam emerged out of desert Arabia, it appropriated much of the religious architecture of the surrounding Christian cultures for its own use. This is not to say, of course, that there were no other influences or that there was not a great deal of creativity in the adaptations themselves. There is, nevertheless, a great deal of commonality. The *mihrāb* or the niche facing Mecca is strongly reminiscent of the apses in Christian churches, the minarets remind us of towers and the term *minbar* which is used for the raised platform from which the sermon is delivered is used also by Christians and, in a slightly varied form, by Jews for the pulpit. The central feature of the mosque, the dome, is, of course, of Byzantine origin. Throughout the centuries, churches have been converted into mosques and, in some cases such as Spain, mosques have been turned into churches. In addition, sacred buildings (such as tombs) belonging to one faith have sometimes been used as places of worship by those of the other faith.[15]

—— *Islam and Inculturation* ——

We have noticed the tremendously wide range of sharing that has existed between Muslims and Christians over the past centuries. This has implications for the inculturation of Christian spirituality in cultures which have been shaped by Islam. Inculturation is a necessary aspect of evangelization. The gospel cannot be said to have been shared unless it is first translated or interpreted into the language, thought-forms and life-style of a particular people. There is an inherent capacity in the gospel for interpretation into a multitude of languages and cultures. Both history and contemporary experience bear witness to this continual process of interpreting the gospel to different ages and cultures. It has been pointed out in this chapter that Islam was itself formed within a Christian milieu and that its subsequent contacts with Christianity have had a formative influence on its spiritual and material culture. The inculturation of the gospel and of Christian spirituality into Islamic cultures thus poses a specially fascinating challenge for Christians. How far is it possible to use Muslim devotional terminology, formed under Christian influence, for contemporary Christian worship? Should common terms be used for God?

Should postures of reverence and meditation be adopted? Is it possible to build churches with domes and minarets? Is it desirable? How may Christian distinctives be communicated in forms which have been used to convey other distinctives?

Different churches and Christians in different situations will come to different conclusions about these matters. What is important, however, is that Christians should take inculturation seriously not only at the level of translating the Scriptures and other Christian literature but in forms of worship, posture at prayer, liturgical terminology, spiritual exercises, and other related matters. Owing to a very long history of interaction, dialogue, and simply living together, Christian inculturation within cultures shaped by Islam has particular significance. In the area of spirituality it can provide the Christian Church with a rich vocabulary and heritage, much of which would be a recovery by the Church of its own past should the Church decide to appropriate it for its own life and witness.[16]

— 10 —

Mission, Dialogue, and Multi-Faith Worship

✳

Awareness among both Jews and Christians that they are communities in covenant with God *has* brought a sense of a certain exclusiveness in their relationships with people of other faiths, especially in the matter of worship. Where Christians are concerned, the two central sacraments of baptism and eucharist are related to Christ's death and resurrection, and represent, on the one hand, the incorporation of believers into Christ and, on the other, his presence in the believing community. From the earliest days, baptism into Christ's body, the Church, has excluded belonging to other religious groups such as the mystery religions of the ancient world.[1] In this sense, Christianity is different from certain other religions. One can, for example, be both a Shintoist and a Buddhist at the same time but, as any Japanese Christian will tell you, one cannot be a Shintoist and a Christian at the same time.[2] Participation in the Eucharist, the remembrance and representation of Christ's death, has also since very early times excluded participation in the sacrificial meals of other religions (1 Cor. 10.14–22).

The situation, however, is not as watertight as some imagine. In Judaism, Gentiles were admitted even into the Temple precincts, although they were restricted to the outermost court. Synagogues, which were gaining in importance even before the destruction of Jerusalem in AD 70, opened their doors to 'God-fearing' Gentiles who wished to join them in worship and in religious discussion. The early preaching of the gospel often took place in contexts such as these (Acts 13.16; 14.1; 17.2; 18.4).[3] In Christian assemblies too it was expected that non-Christians would sometimes attend worship (1 Cor. 14.23,24) and Jas. 2.1–7). We know from Origen that some Christians, at least, continued to frequent Jewish synagogues until well into the third century.[4] At different times and in different places Christians and Muslims too have shared the same or adjacent premises for their own, separate, acts of worship.[5] We need also to remember that Paul's encounter with the Athenians took place in an area which they would have recognized as sacred; and he certainly referred to their cult and quoted from what amounted to their scripture, that is the poets (Acts 17.22–31).

—— God Hears the Prayers of All ——

The Bible appears to teach that the prayers of those outside the convenant-community can be heard by God. Abimelech's prayer was heard (Gen. 20), as were the prayers of the crew of Jonah's ship (Jonah 1.14–16). Jethro's sacrifice (Exod. 18.12) was, presumably, acceptable to God, and there is no indication that Nebuchadnezzar's prayer of thanksgiving was not acceptable (Dan. 4.34–37). The stories of Melchizedek (Gen. 14.18–21) and of Balaam (Num. 22) show us that people outside the covenant-community may exercise a ministry to us and on our behalf. We are also told that God will hear us when we pray for them (Gen. 20.7,17; 1 Kings 17.20–23).

Twenty years ago the Church Pastoral Aid Society published a booklet entitled *Can we pray with the unconverted?* The booklet used some of the biblical passages just quoted in its argument, and came to the conclusion that the Church of England is right to offer its ministry to *all* the people of England, Christian or not, and to pray for them and with them. It seemed particularly to have in mind the occasional offices, for which there is a demand in the general population at times of rites of passage such as birth, marriage, or death.[6] National and civic occasions, when avowedly agnostic or atheistic people participate in the worship of the established Church, must also be included here. On such occasions, the order of worship may be mainly Christian, though readings from literature and pieces of secular music may well be included.

—— Sharing with People of Other Faiths ——

But is what is sauce for the goose also sauce for the gander? If the Church can offer its ministry to people with only a tenuous connection with the Christian faith and can pray with and for those who are avowedly non-Christian, can it also pray with and for those of other faiths?

As a matter of fact, in many countries Christians share a culture with others where the existence of God is assumed and his blessings invoked during the course of ordinary life. People refer to God when they meet each other, before and after meals, and at times of sadness or of celebration. Christians are glad to join in on such occasions because they know the Father of Jesus Christ to be Lord of all and because they know that all people have been vouchsafed *some* knowledge of God, however much it might have been distorted by social and personal sin (Acts 14.17, 17.23; Rom. 1.19–22, 2.1–16).[7]

In the course of Christian mission and ministry, one is likely to be asked to pray with people of another faith in personal and family contexts. At the end of a conversation, religious leaders may well pray for their Christian interlocutor and ask the Christian to pray for them. A Christian may also be asked to pray in a variety of other situations: at mealtimes, at weddings or funerals or in times of civil or military conflict. These are opportunities for showing pastoral concern and also for authentic Christian witness.

At times of national or civic celebrations or mourning, too, Christians may well be asked to participate in events which have a 'religious' aspect to them. Such an aspect may be limited to silent meditation, or it may extend to the reading of various texts and the offering of prayers by people of different faiths. Christians need to be discriminating in their participation in such events and, if they decide to participate, they need to do so in sensitive and appropriate ways. However, if they are not to be marginalized in the social and political life of a community, they cannot easily decline to participate in any form at all.

—— *Limits of Multi-Faith Worship* ——

Christians need to be aware that multi-faith occasions often take place at the level of the lowest common denominator and cannot, therefore, be a substitute for full Christian worship. For these reasons also, this will not be a frequent occurrence in the life of an individual Christian or of a Christian community, but will be reserved for occasions when pastoral sensitivity requires that Christian witness be expressed in this way.

When Christians decide that it is right for them to participate in a multi-faith occasion, they should make sure that they do not acquiesce in anything which is contrary to the Christian faith or which dishonours in any way the person and work of Jesus Christ. They will often discover that people of other faiths are as anxious not to give offence to Christians as Christians are about not offending them.[8]

Multi-faith occasions may well be based on common perceptions of God's universal Lordship, or on more general common perceptions such as 'the ultimacy of the spiritual', but they do not necessarily involve the belief that religious traditions are salvific *of themselves*, nor do they necessarily militate against Christian witness to the universal Lord's unique self-disclosure in Jesus of Nazareth. In fact, they may sometimes be occasions for such witness.

— 11 —

Jesus, Justice, and the Jews

✳

> *How odd of God to choose the Jews!*
> *But odder still of those*
> *who choose a Jewish God*
> *But spurn the Jews!*
> (Ronald Knox)

The history of the Jewish people is largely one of humiliation, oppression and persecution. In Christian Byzantium, and then in medieval Europe, they were in turn discriminated against, persecuted and exiled. They were accused of deicide, that is, they were held to have corporate and continuing responsibility for the Crucifixion, and the 'teaching of contempt' was enshrined in church life. Whatever the nature of the anti-Christian polemic in rabbinic and medieval Judaism, such behaviour among Christians cannot ever be justified.[1]

—— The Holocaust ——

National Socialism had profoundly pagan roots, traceable to the attempts to revive Teutonic paganism in the nineteenth century. As a movement, therefore, it was anti-Christian. In its anti-Semitism, however, it could and did draw on the evil and prejudice left behind by medieval 'Christendom'. The terrible climax to European anti-Semitism was the *Shoah* or Holocaust when millions of European Jews perished in the gas chambers.

Some Jews are beginning to reflect on the theological significance of the *Shoah*. Understandably, there are various responses, ranging from abandonment of belief in God to its reconstruction in a post-holocaust age. Some see it as an instance, perhaps the ultimate instance, of Israel's call to be Yahweh's suffering servant. In this sense, the *Shoah* can be seen as a fulfilment of Israel's call to be obedient to Yahweh to the end. From another, more immediate, point of view, however, it must be seen as one of the greatest crimes against humanity. Its memory will continue to affect the way the world community treats Jews and their aspirations. The ways in which Jews relate to others will also continue to be influenced by memories of the *Shoah*. This is as it should be.[2]

—— The Jews and Islam ——

Nor is the world of Islam innocent in this matter. Along with Christians, Jews, as *ahl al-kitab* (or People of the Book), have had the status of *dimmi* or protected people. This, however, has not prevented their humiliation, persecution and even extermination at the hands of fanatical rulers, *Ulema* (divines) and mobs.[3]

In more tolerant times, again along with Christians, the Jews made a tremendous contribution to learning, trade, and culture in the Islamic world.[4] Their reward as a people, however, was not commensurate. It is to the credit of Islamic civilizations that despite systematic humiliation and periodic persecutions, no atrocity on the scale of the Holocaust can be recorded against them. It is only in a few countries, such as India, however, that the Jews have avoided persecution altogether, have found a welcome and even proselytized![5]

The Jews are right to demand justice from the world, and the world has a moral obligation to see that they, along with other oppressed peoples, get justice. Such justice, however, cannot be at the expense of justice to others. In particular, it cannot be at the expense of those who have lived in the Holy Land for centuries.[6]

—— Jews and the Land ——

The attachment to the land of many (though not all) Jews is very understandable. This is the land which was promised to the Patriarchs, it is the land to which the fleeing Hebrews came at the time of the Exodus; the Davidic Kingship and the Temple of Solomon were established here. We need to note, however, that the continued possession of the land is conditional on the Israelites keeping *their* part of the Covenant.

The Old Testament makes it abundantly clear that covenants can be broken and many of the prophetic warnings about exile are based on the realization that the people of Israel have yet again broken their covenant with Yahweh. Indeed, Jeremiah regards the Covenant as so completely broken that a new one is needed to replace it (Jer. 31.31). Although the reference here is primarily to the Sinaitic Covenant, we need to remember that Jeremiah's prophetic work took place in the context of imminent exile from the land.

The last great dispersion of the Jews from the Holy Land began after the failure of Bar Cochba's revolt in AD 135 and continued until the end of the fourth century AD. For many centuries, Jews have lived in many lands all over the world. They have learnt to make these lands their own. Not only have they been 'assimilated' into the local cultures, they have made notable contributions to them.

Contrary to popular belief, Judaism has been an actively proselytizing faith at particular times and in certain places. The question 'who is a Jew?' is at least as difficult to answer as the question 'who is an Arab?' While there is a certain cultural and racial continuity among Jewish communities, a simple 'right to return' ideology fails to take account of the real ethnic and cultural diversity.[7]

How Jewish are the *Falasha* of Ethiopia or the *Bani Israil* of Bombay? A significant number of recent Soviet immigrants to Israel are thought to be Gentiles taking the chance to get out of the Soviet Union! Many are now being instructed in the Jewish faith. Indeed, it is possible for anyone to be instructed by an Orthodox rabbi, to convert to Judaism and to acquire the 'right to return' to Israel!

—— The Bible and Israel ——

From the Christian point of view, biblical interpretation that sees in the return of the Jews to the Holy Land a fulfilment of prophecy is largely an innovation of nineteenth-century literalism. Such a literalism was decisively rejected by CMS leaders such as Thomas Scott and Charles Simeon. Traditional interpretation has in part seen such prophecy as already fulfilled (as, for example, in the return from Babylon) and in part as being fulfilled in the Church and among Jewish people in terms of their spiritual destiny.

It is hazardous, therefore, to make a case for the return of the Jews to the land in terms of biblical prophecy. The centrality of the land in the Jewish faith and in Jewish devotion and expectations, however, leads us to view with sympathy the claim that Jews should have guaranteed and secure access to the Holy Land, that this can only be achieved if there is a substantial Jewish presence there and if the Jews have some power to make such access secure.[8]

Such a position does *not* necessarily entail a belief in Zionism. Jews could have such a presence, for example in a unitary state where they lived together with Muslims, Christians, and Druze. In terms of contemporary *realpolitik*, such a presence could also be secured by partitioning the land into separate Jewish and Palestinian states.

—— The New Testament, Christians and Jews ——

Although the New Testament is innocent of any reflection on Israel
and the land, it does affirm that, despite the new covenant in Jesus,
God has a continuing and gracious purpose for his ancient people.
Romans chapters 9—11 is rightly seen as the key passage here. Paul
acknowledges the call and heritage of Israel and he looks forward to
the time when all Israel will recognize their Messiah. In the meantime,
Christians are to respect the Jews as the source from which much of
their faith comes and as especially chosen by God as witnesses to his
mighty works.

Indeed, as the Second Vatican Council reminds us, the Church
needs to understand Israel if she is to understand herself! Every aspect
of the Christian life – worship, teaching, preaching and service – is
permeated with the patrimony which the Church has received from
Israel.[9] This becomes clear when a Christian attends a Christian service
with a Jewish friend. It is also worth noting how much we owe to the
Jewish *Birkath Hammazon* (Blessing for Food) in the development of the
Eucharist.[10]

In our worship, preaching, and teaching we need to acknowledge
this debt. There is also a need to counter the deep-seated prejudices
created by centuries of 'the teaching of contempt'. It is true that the
Jewish authorities of the day pressed for the death of Jesus and that the
mob took responsibility for this heinous act. But natural justice
demands that we should not extend this culpability to *all* Jews of that
time and of later times. The 1988 Lambeth Conference has reminded
us that Christian preaching, particularly during Lent and Holy Week,
should take special care to avoid any suggestion which might be
understood in an anti-Semitic way.[11]

—— The Universality of Christ and of —— Christian Mission

While Scripture teaches that God has a continuing purpose for the
Jews, it is also clear that this purpose is fulfilled in Christ. There can be
no radical separation of 'the two ways'. Christ is the Saviour of all: 'the
Jew first and also the Greek'. Although the New Testament always has
the dimension of universality in view, it does not countenance the view
that the Christian mission is simply about opening the Covenant to the
Gentiles.[12]

The ministry of Jesus himself was overwhelmingly among Jews and it was they who recognized him as one who taught with authority. The disciples were sent first to 'the lost sheep of the House of Israel' (Matt. 10.6). Even at the time of receiving their universal commission they were told to begin in Jerusalem and Judaea (Acts 1.8). Needless to say, the early disciples were all Jews and their first converts were Jews, including 'a great many priests' (Acts 6.7). Even Paul began his preaching among Jews and only later extended it to the Gentiles (Acts 13.46, 1 Cor. 9.20–21).

It is perhaps worth noting that Jesus accepted the title of 'Messiah' with great reserve *precisely* because his view of his own person and ministry differed markedly from common Jewish expectations of the Messiah – although, it must be said, both he and the early Church could see continuities as well.[13]

—— *Jewish Christians* ——

From Origen, we know that there were many Jewish Christians in third-century Palestine who were at the synagogue on the Sabbath and in church on the Lord's Day. In addition, there were sects of Jewish Christians, such as the Ebionites, who did not mix with Gentile Christians, in order to preserve their Jewishness. In fact, throughout Christian history there have been Jewish Christians who have come to acknowledge Jesus of Nazareth as their Messiah, but have also greatly valued their Jewish heritage. Our present age is no exception. There are many Jewish Christians in the main Christian churches and, in addition, there are communities of 'Messianic believers' as well.

We greet with joy and love all such brothers and sisters and note with sadness that it is often difficult for them even to be acknowledged as Jews by their kinsfolk. It is ironical that one can be an atheist or agnostic and be accepted as a Jew, and yet Jewish Christians often do not find such acceptance. The Church as a whole can learn a very great deal from Jewish Christians and it is vital that barriers to fellowship between Gentiles and Jews should not be erected in the name of contextualization.

It is right, of course, that Jewish Christians should seek to express and to live their faith in the context of their culture and their religious background. This cannot, however, be at the expense of the gospel and fellowship between Christians and churches. It is perhaps worth noting that not a single one of the early Jewish Christian sects has survived. Jewish Christians need their Gentile brothers and sisters just as much as their Gentile brothers and sisters need them.

Evangelization, Dialogue and People of Other Faiths

Some Jewish leaders are asking for assurances that in the Decade of Evangelism the Churches will seek only to evangelize 'nominal' Christians. This cannot be if the Church is to be faithful to the universality of the gospel. The gospel has to be proclaimed to the whole of creation. This has to be done sensitively and with the greatest of respect for all human beings, and especially for those of other faiths.

Christians need to listen carefully and at length to others, they need to learn from others and to respect their freedom of belief. At the same time, they need to share the good news of God's revelation of himself in Christ. If Christ is the definitive 'clue' to the Father and his love, if Christians have experienced God's love and power through Christ, if the Church is a community of forgiveness and reconciliation, Christians will be compelled to share the gospel with others, whether they be Jews or Gentiles, 'nominal' Christians or people of other faiths.

In the spirit of dialogue, Christians will want to affirm all that is good and true in the lives of non-believers as well as in the lives of those of other faiths. But they will find both the source and the fulfilment of all goodness and truth in Christ, the Eternal Word of God.

Christians will renounce all kinds of pressure and inducements when inviting others to consider the claims of Christ. In particular, they will avoid the direct targeting of 'vulnerable' groups such as the children of other faith-communities. It is especially important that in the matter of evangelization Christians should be on guard against the sin of *hubris* and everything should be done in the humility which we have seen in the one who, though in the form of God, emptied himself and took the form of a slave.

> . . . to them belong the sonship, the glory, the covenants, the giving of the law, the worship and the promises; to them belong the patriarchs, and of their race, according to the flesh, is the Christ. God who is over all be blessed for ever. Amen.

— 12 —
Where Is Christ To Be Found Today?

*

This is a difficult subject to tackle, and I did have to consider where to begin. There are so many bright spirits who see Christ everywhere and, while one can applaud their optimism and their enthusiasm, one can't say the same about their judgement! On the other hand, there are people who see Christ along a very narrow trajectory indeed, and this tunnel vision seriously and adversely affects their outreach.

I want to begin with asking how it is that the Christic question is asked in various traditions and cultures? What I mean is, the kinds of questions that Christians find answered in Jesus Christ, how are these questions even asked and how are they answered in other traditions? Historically speaking, many systems of belief recognize both the phenomenal world with its changes and chances, and an unchanging absolute which is the source and the ground of the world's being and which cannot simply be identified with it. That is common over a whole range of thinking and of religion. At the same time, such an absolute as source, ground, and sustainer of the world's being needs also to be related to it. Now the problem that has often arisen in world religions is how this can be possible without compromising the absoluteness of the absolute, as it were. That is, how this can be possible without relativizing the absolute, making it simply part of the phenomenal world of which it is ground. On the other hand, there is the opposite danger of absolutizing the world and denying its contingent character altogether. The one kind of exercise results in an unprincipled pluralism where the universe lacks ground, cause, or foundation, and the other is a lapse into an undifferentiated monism where the universe lacks any independent existence at all. This much is common in many systems.

The Need for a Mediator

Now different religions and philosophical systems have developed the idea of a mediator between the one and the many, the absolute and the relative, God and the world. Such a mediator shares in the nature of God, but also sums up, or recapitulates, the world. It is interesting to note how often the mediator is understood as thought, word, or act: an externalization, as it were, of the absolute being that brings the world into existence and sustains it at every moment without compromising the transcendence of the absolute. So the Christic question is not only beginning to be asked but also to be answered. Thus in Hinduism, if Brahman is the eternal absolute, utterly transcendent and beyond predication of any kind, then *I'svara* is the externalization, the personal aspect of Brahman, responsible for the world's creation and its return to Brahman the absolute. Father Raimundo Pannikar has most ably provided a Christian commentary on this view, and has also pointed out its importance as *preparatio evangelica* as far as Christian mission is concerned.[1] In Hellenistic thought the Logos, as you know, was understood as the divine reason, which has brought the universe into being, and provided it with order while at the same time illumining the minds of human beings and enabling them to understand their world, themselves and God. Its importance for later Christian thought is too well-known to need repetition. Even in faith traditions where there is a strong emphasis on a personal God, the need to safeguard divine transcendence often results in the recognition of a mediator, sometimes the hypostatized word or command of God. This word or command of God is seen as manifesting God's power in the world and in the human mind. In the Old Testament the term *Dabar* is already beginning to acquire such a meaning, notably in Psalms 33 and 107. This is developed in later Jewish writings in the use of the term *Memra*. Once again the importance of Christian theology is well known. *Memra* is etymologically related to the Arabic *Amr* which is referred to in the Qur'ān as Allah's command (Qur'ān 17.85 the *Surah* called The Children of Israel). Bishop Kenneth Cragg has pointed out that in Muslim thought this is understood as the divine *Amr* by which the world has come into being and by which it is sustained.[2] Many religious systems, only too aware of human fallenness and the selfishness which results from it, see the need for revelation if this relationship between God and the world is to be appreciated. Thus in Hindu tradition, the intuition that Brahman is transcendent and yet the world's cause in *I'svara* comes from a realization by the wise men, the *rishis*, that can only be described as revelation. That is why this insight is preserved, according to Hindus, in the sacred writings.[3] In a very different context, the divine *Amr* of the Qur'ān is that which makes God's will known to human beings as well as being the cause of the world's being.[4]

——— *Jesus Christ the Mediator* ———

This apprehension in so many different contexts that the world is related to God by a mediator who may be described as God's thought, word or act is, Christians believe, definitively revealed in the living, the dying and the rising again of Jesus of Nazareth. This is the *Christological criterion* by which all truth, goodness, and beauty are to be known and judged. When we wish to see how God has been preparing different people, cultures, movements, religious traditions, and even counter religious movements for his kingdom, we need to examine their values, beliefs, and communal structures in the light of this criterion. Only insofar as these are seen as consonant with the revelation in Christ can they be seen as having salvific value in God's work of preparing all for salvation in Christ. Now there are some, like John Hick, who would refuse to use this Christological criterion, claiming that it puts salvation in Christ at the centre rather than something like the universal salvific will of God. But the axiom of God's universal love and desire to save all people is known to us in Christ. As Gavin D'Costa has pointed out, the pluralist position presupposes that we know something to be true while denying the validity and normative status of those events that reveal and are part of that truth.[5] It is a circular argument, in other words.

So the axiom of God's universal love and desire to save all people is known to us in Christ, and we might extend that a little and say that it is known to us through saving history, through the history of God's revelation of himself in the events in Israel and in Jesus Christ. But we could perhaps push it back a little further, as do the Jewish people in their view of universalism, to the covenant with Noah. But however far back we push it, we still begin with some kind of revelation, and it is this that allows us to see other events in this world in the light of God's purposes. To put Christ at the centre then, is not to deny that God is at work in many and wonderful ways through his creation. As John Robinson has said (quoting Sloane Coffin), 'to believe that God is best defined by Christ is not to believe that God is confined to Christ'.[6]

—— *Trinitarian Inclusiveness* ——

Now are there other theological grounds for applying this Christologi-cal criterion? Christians have often seen perceptions of truth, practice of goodness and appreciation of beauty among human beings as rooted in the biblical teaching that all human beings have been made in the image of God, that in spite of its awful reality, sin has not destroyed this image, though its *has* become tarnished and obscured. The teaching of the New Testament is that it is Christ who is pre-eminently the image of the invisible God. The term 'icon' is used by St Paul both in the Corinthian correspondence and in Colossians, and 'icon' evokes the term used in Genesis which is *selem*, something that is carved out. Human beings participate in this, in Christ as the image of God, to the extent that they have been created by Christ and are held together in him. This is the burden of Paul's argument in Colossians. Of course, such a participation in Christ is greatly enhanced, as Karl Rahner saw, for those who acknowledge the Eternal Word as definitively revealed in Jesus and become members of that social manifestation of such belonging, the Church. In other words, participation in Christ through baptism into the Church is not a difference in kind but of degree compared to other human beings outside the Church. The Eternal Word, incarnate in Jesus Christ, enlightens all human beings (John 1.9) and God has not left himself without witness anywhere.[7] In the early Church, when Christians began to deal with the cult and the philosophies and the cultures around them, they seized on this idea of the divine Logos enlightening all human beings as a point of departure in their thinking about the world outside.

We have seen that the Early Fathers, such as Justin Martyr and Clement of Alexandria, saw the work of the divine Logos first as exposing *falsehood*; so the falsehoods of the mystery religions were exposed by the light of the Eternal Word. But, second, both Justin and Clement saw the divine Logos as *revealing truth*, in the poetry of the ancient Greeks, for instance, as arguably St Paul had already done at Athens. We must remember, of course, that poetry for the Greeks was almost like scripture; it was seen as inspired. They saw the work, then, of the divine Logos in poetry, in Hellenistic *philosophy* insofar as it witnessed to the truths of Christian revelation, in the *practical morality* of the Stoics and even, this is quite remarkable, in the so-called *prophetic oracles* of the pagans, as far as they seemed to them to witness to Christ. Now we know that some of these oracles had, by the time Clement got to see them, already been under Christian influence, but the point is that Clement did not know this, he took them as pagan and evaluated them on that basis.[8] So we have God's image, pre-eminently Christ and by participation all human beings, the Eternal Word enlightening all human beings, and God's Spirit at work in the world, bringing human beings to a realization of their own sin, their brokenness before God and so to repentance and forgiveness. It is this, Sir Norman Anderson has pointed out, that is significant about spirituality among people of other faiths, not their goodness or even the content of their religion, but whether the Spirit can bring such people to a realization of their own sin, their brokenness before God and to repentance.[9] *The economy of the Holy Spirit* (that, of course, is a term used by the Orthodox), according to Archbishop Georges Khodr of Mount Lebanon, is such that the Spirit is present everywhere and fills everything. The work of the Spirit, moreover, is to witness to Christ and to fashion Christ in the hearts and minds of men and women everywhere.[10] So that is how the Christological criterion might work with these supplementary criteria, as it were, to support it.

——— *Where May Christ Be Found Today?* ———

Where then, in the light of these criteria, may Christ be found today as we look around our world? First, we can say that Christ may be found in those aspects of the wisdom, the values and social structures of cultures which enhance the quality of human life and promote truth and love. For example, in the doctrine of *Ahimsa*, or non-violence, which is so dominant a part of Hindu ethos, or possibly in the eight-fold path of the Buddha, or in the social equality of Islam or of Sikhism, which sometimes puts Christians to shame. Second, Christ may be found in movements for liberation that seek to free the oppressed from their misery. For example, the Church's struggle against apartheid in Southern Africa and Gandhi's movement of *Satyagraha*, holding on to truth, the movement for non-violent political and social change. And then, third, Christ may be found in various religious traditions. Now this can happen in several ways. First, Jesus Christ may be explicitly acknowledged. This happens, for example, in Islam. Here his virginal birth, some kinds of accounts of his teaching, his miracles and his glorification are all acknowledged. Some even claim that his death and resurrection are referred to in the Qur'ān, and there is a certain amount of linguistic evidence for that. He is certainly given titles such as Messiah, Word of Truth (*Qawl Al-Haqq*), Word of God (*Kalimatullah*), and Spirit from God (*Ruh^un Min^hu*). So there is the *acknowledged* Christ of Islam and a great deal of dialogue with Muslims can be conducted on the basis of this acknowledged Christ of the Qur'ān and of Muslim devotion and spirituality, especially in the Sufi tradition.[11]

But then in religious traditions there may be the *unacknowledged* presence of Christ in beliefs, in devotion or in practice. The Christological criterion will enable us to discern in each case what it is that is disposing men and women towards repentance of sin and trust in God. This is the unacknowledged Christ of a particular tradition. Although there is an unacknowledged Christ present in some kinds of Hindu reflection and devotion, for example in the Vedanta, there is also an acknowledged Christ vis-à-vis Hinduism in a way very different from Islam. This has to do with the historical encounter of Hinduism and Christianity. Now this encounter goes back to the emergence of the Syrian Indian churches in the early years of Christian history, churches which continue to have a particular witness in India today. But this encounter became much more intense with arrival of Christians from the West and created a ferment in Hinduism. In the end it brought about major reforms within it to such an extent that M. M. Thomas, a leading Indian theologian, can say that modern Hinduism has been remade as a result of encounter with Christianity, for example, in its attitude to caste and in attitudes towards women. In all of these ways Hinduism has changed and this change is acknowledged by major Hindu reformers such as Raja Ram Mohan Roy, Rabindranath Tagore and Mahatma Gandhi.[12] Now the question that arises here is a question that was asked in the 1960s by Bishop John V. Taylor, when he was still General Secretary of CMS, and it is a question that we must ask ourselves again and again. The question is, 'What is the significance of the transformation that results in religious traditions as a consequence of the Church's preaching of Christ?' In other words, we often talk about individual conversion, and rightly so; we even talk about communities of people, villages, becoming Christian in some way. But what about the *transformation of religious traditions as a whole*? This undoubtedly happens and in Hinduism there is a well documented case where it has happened to a very significant extent. I was once with a bishop in South India at Easter time and he took me to a baptism where he baptized some two hundred people. On the way back I was commenting on this, and he told me that this was only the tip of the iceberg, because people who take this step of baptism in India are a very small minority. There is a much larger number for whom Christ is the only Saviour but who remain culturally Hindu, and then there is an even larger number of people for whom Christ has some place, a very important place, but who do not see him as unique! So it is very difficult in India to tell how this transformation comes about and to pinpoint it, but that it occurs cannot be doubted. Now having said all of this, we need to note also that there is a down or negative side to religion. While in some aspects of it we may be able to discern the life of the Eternal Word and the work of the Holy Spirit, there are other aspects where this is not the case. The repression of women, barbarous penal codes, the caste system, so-called holy wars, all of these show the unattractive side of religion. When the gospel is brought to bear on this side of religion there can only be judgement and a call for repentance.

The Gospel and Our Culture movement has rightly criticized the Enlightenment and the movements which flowed from it as tending to be reductionist. The cosmos is reduced to a mechanism, the spiritual realm is rendered unknowable, and religion is consigned to the values and beliefs which people may hold in private. This much is true, but it is not the whole story. Secularity too is a culture and the missionary lesson is that it must be treated like any other culture, and like any culture when the gospel is brought to an encounter with it, there are aspects of it which are judged and other aspects which are affirmed. This is perhaps something that the Gospel and Our Culture movement has not taken seriously enough. Many in modern science today, for example, are struck by the law and order of the universal process. They are impressed, moreover, by the correspondence there is between the process and the workings of our own minds. Professor John Polkinghorne often tells us that the more simple and elegant a scientific theory is, the more likely it is to be true. It is interesting that Paul Davies' book, which opens up the question of science's relationship to religion from a scientist's point of view, is called *The Mind of God*.[13] Surely here, if anywhere, Christians should see the illuminating work of the Eternal Word, the mind or reason of God. Nor need such a way of understanding God's relationship with the world be necessarily deistic. In spite of all the dangers in adopting such a position, surely we must allow that our own experience of freedom in interacting with our environment must be true also of God, only infinitely more so? The incarnation would then be seen as a unique instance of such interaction and yet also as providing clues for the discernment of this interaction elsewhere. We are back to the Christological criterion.

———— *Art and Transcendence* ————

Art and literature too are areas where the presence or absence of God is continually being debated. Some, like George Steiner, regard all art as a manifestation of the transcendent, others have devoted their creativity to a search for the transcendent. Stephen Metcalf in his obituary of William Golding tells us that throughout his life Golding was driven to discover and rediscover two things; that *Homo sapiens* is and, so far as we have record, always has been heroic but sick, and that hidden behind the darkness within or else revealed against *Homo sapiens* and incommensurably more worthy of attention is *God*! According to Metcalf, Golding saw men and women as both fallen *and* in the image of God, as rebellious, and yet, as capable of receiving divine revelation. Surely, we must see the Divine Word and the Holy Spirit at work in the artist's and the author's agonizing search for truth?[14] Some years ago I was confirming at Magdalen College, Oxford. Talking to the confirmands before the service began, I was struck that several of them said that they had come to faith through the ministry of the choir! So many parish clergy are deeply aware of the place of music in bringing many to an awareness of a world beyond the everyday one of business, family and civic responsibility.

What significance does this have for the Church's task today and where is Christ to be found in this world? The widespread humanism in the contemporary world, which is seen in the recognition of the dignity of all human beings, and which is the basis for so many charitable appeals, is also worthy of note. What is it that gives Comic Relief the energy that it has? Surely a gospel which teaches that human beings are made in the image of God, an image moreover which he restores and perfects in them, has something to say to contemporary humanism, however imperfect it may be. The Church's mission is to discern the presence of Christ and his grace and truth in men and women everywhere. It is then to declare him as definitively revealed in Jesus of Nazareth, but in terms that are intelligible to people, and which resonate with the truth they have already. It is here that the extent of God's preparation of a people or a person can become clear. As John Taylor has put it, the Spirit at work in the evangelist is also the Spirit at work in the one being evangelized.[15] The Christ who is proclaimed is also the Christ who is perhaps dimly, but deeply, recognized as the source and ground of one's being, thought, and love. The Church's mission also has an eschatological dimension to it. It is to seek for the fulfilment of all things in Christ, to pray for the coming of the Kingdom when the divine purpose will be disclosed in its fullness. In the meanwhile, the Church perceives, encounters and handles all human institutions and achievements in the light of the judgement that the gospel brings to them, but also in the knowledge that God's purposes are being worked out in them and through them, and that their final destiny is in the hands of the Living God.

— 13 —

Jesus Christ:
The Light of the World

＊

—— The Uniqueness of Christ ——

In the 1980s the word 'choice' became very important. People spoke of the need to exercise choice where their personal relationships were concerned, for example, or of choice about where they were to educate their children, or of choice in matters of health. I suspect that this word 'choice' and how people are to have choice in this world will continue to be important for us, but it is also a word that is very important in the Bible. *God* chooses: God chooses groups of people and, indeed, God chooses individuals through whom to reveal himself to the world and to reveal his will for us.

Consider the way in which God chose the people of Israel at a time when they were not at all a significant force. They were enslaved, despised, and obscure. But God chose them and delivered them from their bondage in Egypt to reveal his power to the world.[1] Think of the prophets, how God chose them and how remarkably reluctant many of them were to be chosen! Remember all the excuses they gave: 'I am not really a prophet by descent', 'I am a husbandman', 'I am too young'. All these excuses were put forward and yet God chose these prophets to declare his will to his people.

But the most important choice of all is, of course, God's choice of his eternal Son, his Eternal Word, his mind, his reason – we can translate *Logos* in all those ways – to reveal himself finally, definitively, adequately, sufficiently to the world.

Choosing the Ordinary

Now, for some people, this particularity of choice is a difficulty. They ask why God, if he is the God of the universe, if he is the God of all human beings everywhere, expresses himself through particular people. Does this not compromise his universality?

I want to state, first of all, that although the choice of God's Eternal Word is in a category by itself – he is chosen because he is near to God and reveals God in a way that no one else can – the choice of human beings, whether singly or in groups, is despite their being very ordinary. The people of Israel were not chosen because they were special but they became special because they were chosen. At the time they were chosen, there was nothing about them that would attract people to them.

The same can be said of the prophets and, indeed, of the time, place, culture and humanity which the Eternal Word took at the time of the incarnation. Indeed, that is its value: 'Our Lord Jesus Christ though he was rich, yet for our sake he became poor' (2 Cor. 8.9). God chooses ordinary things and ordinary people to express his will to us.

I have often understood this as like the work of an artist, of a painter or a sculptor. When painters want to paint, they will choose a piece of material on which to paint – that may be a piece of canvas – and they will express themselves on that piece of canvas. Similarly, when sculptors want to sculpt, they will choose a piece of wood or metal or whatever it is. Now this material in itself has no intrinsic value. But once the artist has expressed himself or herself through that material, then it becomes very valuable and people will pay hundreds of thousands of pounds for such pieces of art. God's choice of the ordinary, his use of the ordinary, is a bit like that. We are nothing in ourselves, but by and through God's choice we can do mighty things.

SUPERNATURAL AUTHORITY

Jesus was greatly conscious of the presence of God in him and of God's work through him. He was conscious of the supernatural authority which he had received from his Father, and not only he but those around him were conscious of this authority. 'What is this?' they said, 'a new teaching! He teaches with authority and not as the scribes and the Pharisees' (cf Matt. 7.29).

This authority that Jesus felt, and which others around him felt, is seen in his *teaching*, his *healing*, his *feeding*, and his *forgiving*. Let us take the *teaching* first. The originality of the teaching of Jesus to be found in the Gospels is such that is has survived more than a hundred years now of rigorous criticism of the Bible and we are still in a position to say that if someone could prove that Jesus Christ did not exist at all, then we would have to invent a very remarkable person who brought this very remarkable teaching.

In my ministry among Muslims, in particular, I have often found that people are attracted to Jesus first because of this teaching – teaching about relationships, about marriage, about forgiveness, about the interior life, about so many things. Supernatural authority is discernible in his teaching, and then in the great works that he did, the *healings* and the *feedings*.

Again, people, both disciples and enemies of Jesus, could see this power in Christ and it is interesting that, both in the New Testament and beyond, the enemies of Jesus could not deny that he had the power to heal. They could say that the origins of this power were from elsewhere, ascribe it to the Devil, perhaps. We find that, even in the second and third centuries, the opponents of the Christians do not deny that Jesus had this power but try to ascribe it to a different source.

There was authority in his healing and in his feeding. I will deal shortly with the authority of his forgiving. Jesus had a sense of supernatural authority, but then, second, he had a sense of fulfilment of prophecy in his life, and not only he but those around him recognized it too.

THE CLIMAX OF HUMAN HISTORY

I suppose that, among all the ancient peoples, the Jewish people were unique in having a view of history which saw it as coming to a climax. Many other ancient peoples had a view of human life and of history which was cyclical. The Bible is unique in ancient literature in having a different view of history. This coming to a climax of human history, as it is portrayed in the Bible, is spoken of as the coming of God himself. The favourite expression of the prophets is 'the day of the Lord' – when the Lord comes. And already in the Old Testament, I believe, this coming of the Lord is beginning to be associated with a human figure.

This human figure is sometimes the Messiah, as in Psalm 2.7: 'You are my son, today I have begotten you.' In the season of Advent we think of those great prophecies in Isaiah where the coming Davidic Messiah is spoken of as the 'mighty God', or the 'divine hero' as one translation puts it (Isa. 9.6). In Ezekiel, God promises his people that he will come as their shepherd and the passage immediately speaks of the Messiah as the shepherd of the people of God (Ezek. 34). And then we have the figure of the divine Son of Man to whom all authority and dominion and power is given (Dan.7.13–14).

Jesus, of course, used the title 'Messiah' with great reserve because it was apt to be misunderstood by the people of his day, but he did agree with his disciples when they ascribed it to him and certainly he understood his ministry in terms of some of the prophecies having to do with the coming of the Messiah.

THE COMING OF GOD

His most typical title for himself, 'the Son of Man', is not so much about his humanity as about the divine authority that he has received.[2]

But he goes further than that and in the first three Gospels, as well as in the Gospel according to St John, he is shown as going much further than that. He ascribes prophecies that are about the coming of Yahweh, the God of Israel, to his own life and ministry. Think of the time when the disciples of John came to Jesus and said, 'Are you the one who is to come or should we look for another?' and Jesus said, 'Look around you, the lame are walking, the deaf are hearing, the blind see, captives are liberated. Go and tell John what you have seen' (Matt. 11.2–6). If we look back to the thirty-fifth chapter of the book of the prophet Isaiah, we will see that this is a prophecy about the coming of Yahweh, the coming of God himself; that when God comes, these things will happen. And Jesus is clearly associating this prophecy with his own ministry.

Then, talking again about John the Baptist, he said, 'Elijah has come if you can accept such a saying.' And people have thought that perhaps this saying is primarily about John the Baptist. It is, of course, about him, but if we look at the very last part of the Old Testament, in the book of the prophet Malachi, the coming of Elijah precedes the coming of God, and Jesus saying 'accept this if you can' is not so much about John being Elijah as about Jesus being God – the fulfilment of prophecy!

UNION WITH THE FATHER

Jesus is conscious that his authority comes from his close intimacy with his Father. Once again, the first three Gospels are as strong about this as that of St John: 'All things have been given to me by my Father; and no one knows the Son except the Father, and no one knows the Father but the Son and those to whom the Son reveals him' (Matt. 11.27). Again and again we find that the source of his authority, the source of his power, is in the intimacy of his union with his Father.

Consider the way in which Jesus accepts his death. There are many things to be said about the significance of the cross, but, for now, think of the way in which he accepted his death. There are many examples from many different cultures and many different ages of people accepting death heroically, accepting death, tragic death, with calmness and courage. For example, Socrates accepted death in a calm and stoical manner. But what has always impressed me about the Passion of our Lord is that at the time of his greatest agony he was able to *forgive* his executioners.

SOMETHING OF A MIRACLE

Think of the resurrection: we may know all the arguments about the resurrection, and all the arguments about why the tomb was empty. Many people have begun to investigate the phenomena surrounding the resurrection with a sceptical frame of mind, but as they have examined the story of the resurrection they have come to believe in its truth.

It is a kind of a miracle that there was a tomb at all. It was not the custom of Roman authorities to provide one. The common fate of criminals crucified was to be flung into a common grave and if Jesus had been flung into a common grave for criminals, any story of the resurrection would have been impossible because the opponents of the disciples could quite easily have pointed out that he had been flung into the pit with common criminals. So the fact of there being a tomb at all is something of a miracle. It underlines the uniqueness of Jesus Christ.[3]

—— *The Universality of Sin* ——

Let us turn now to *the universality of sin*. There have always been religions with religious people who have believed in the perfectibility of men and women, who have believed that people are essentially good and that it is possible through self-improvement to become better, even perfect. This is not an analysis that Christians can make, however, because one of the central teachings of the New Testament is that human beings are not only sinful incidentally, as it were, but that we are caught in a web of sin, by inheritance, environment and inclination, and that we of ourselves cannot escape from this web of sin.[4]

In today's world there are many resurgent religions and new religions which are, once again, teaching the perfectibility of man and of woman. They feel that by teaching people the truths that we have gained, perhaps from the scientists, perhaps from ancient wisdom, we can produce good human societies and good individuals.

Christians will sympathize, of course, with such endeavours, but they will not agree with them because, in the end, the whole Christian story of redemption depends on a proper analysis of the sinfulness of the world, of human society. Human beings could not save themselves, cannot save themselves, therefore the provision of a Saviour is necessary.

GOD'S GRACIOUS PROVISION

So the uniqueness of Christ lies not only in the fact that he is God's revelation for us, in authority and power and in the accepting of death at the hands of sinful human beings, but he is also God's provision for us in the recreation of humanity. 'A second Adam to the fight and to the rescue came' – one who undoes the sin of Adam, who does what Adam could not do and has not done – the new human being. The death of Jesus is significant, is central to human concerns, because it is a death which comes about as a result of creating a new obedient humanity in place of the old.

And this is the invitation of the gospel: we are invited, each one of us, all human beings, to join in solidarity with this new humanity that has come into being, to be behind Jesus, to be 'followers of the Way' – that's a good old CMS expression but it is also one of the earliest names for Christians.

To be with Jesus and in Jesus, united with him and therefore made new – that is really the key to understanding the biblical doctrines of justification and sanctification. We are unable to save ourselves, we are saved by God's gracious provision.

The Uniqueness of Sinners

Then there is *the uniqueness of sinners*. Christians must always, in every place, in every age, distinguish between the sin and the sinner. While we can see that we human beings are caught in a web of personal and social sin, we also know that we are made in the image of God. This image has been distorted and obscured by our sin, but it is still there; that is what makes redemption possible, that is what makes God's project of having created humanity worthwhile and worth redeeming.

Human beings are made in the image of God, and that image has survived our sin. So the good that we see in our neighbours, the good that we from time to time see in ourselves, our strivings for spiritual knowledge, our strivings to worship God in a way worthy of him; all these can be ascribed to the survival of the image of God in us.

But it is not only that the image of God has survived in us, it is also that the Eternal Word, whom we recognize in the face of Jesus Christ, is the same Eternal Word who enlightens all human beings who come into the world.

THE WORK OF THE SPIRIT

God has not left himself without witness anywhere (Acts 14.17). Not only does the Eternal Word enlighten human beings wherever they are – and the early Fathers were quite able to discern the activity of the Eternal Word in whatever was good about humanity, in philosophy or in art or even in poetry – not only does the Eternal Word enlighten all human cultures and is the true source of their achievement, but God's Holy Spirit is at work in the world.

There is a tendency sometimes for Christians to speak as if the Holy Spirit were a personal possession of individual Christians or the corporate possession of the Church. This is not so. The teaching of the Bible is that the Holy Spirit is in the world, convincing the world of sin and righteousness and judgement.

In fact, were it not for this prior work of the Holy Spirit it would not be possible for anyone ever to be converted. It is the Holy Spirit that brings about conversion to God and we are only the means.

So although human beings are fallen sinners, they are also unique because they have been made in the image of God, because God has not left himself without witness and because the Holy Spirit is working in all human beings, bringing them, impelling them, to a knowledge of God.

—— *The Universality of Salvation* ——

Now let us look at *the universality of salvation*: to recap, the Uniqueness of Christ, the Universality of Sin, the Uniqueness of Sinners and the Universality of Salvation. There *is* such a thing as a proper biblical universalism. The Bible teaches that the God who has made heaven and earth, who has made all men and women and children, is the God who is concerned for the ultimate destiny of each one of us. He works for the salvation of all human beings, and this we see focused in the costly work of Christ, not only on the cross but throughout his ministry – the reconciliation of rebellious men and women to God.

God wants all human beings to be saved. And there are many passages in the Old and New Testaments that speak of this desire of God and of his determination to bring it to fulfilment when every knee will bow, every tongue will confess Jesus Christ as Lord. Think of the great images in the Book of Revelation where people from every tribe and nation and tongue are there at the end worshipping God (Rev. 7.9–12).

LOVE AND HUMAN FREEDOM

If there is such a thing as biblical universalism, there is also a tension in the Bible between this desire of God to save all human beings and the freedom that he has given us. He wants us to respond to him in love, and love is something that can only be given freely, you cannot coerce a response of love. And so, it is possible that there are people who reject God's love now and will continue to reject it.

Bishop John Robinson, in a marvellous commentary on the Epistle to the Romans called *Wrestling with Romans*, said God is only love but those who turn away from this love, experience it as wrath. I think that is it in a nutshell.[5]

It is possible for us to continue to turn away from divine love and divine grace because human freedom is as much of a reality as God's will to save us. And so biblical universalism is tempered by this realism, by the possibility of people turning away even from God's love.

EFFECTIVE PRESENTATION

But what of those who have not heard or have not understood? They may not have heard because we have not gone, they may not have understood because our witness has been inadequate. We have been hidebound by our own culture and our own prejudices and have not been able to present the gospel effectively. This is the kind of sixty-four-thousand-dollar question that interviewers love to ask people on programmes on the World Service.

I think we must begin by saying that no one can save himself or herself. We cannot save ourselves, that is absolutely basic to the gospel, but it is also basic to the gospel that God can save us.

OUTSIDE THE CHURCH

What will happen to those who have not heard or have not understood? As we have seen, Sir Norman Anderson, who is well known in this country and throughout the world, used to say that God's revelation of himself in the light of the Eternal Word and the work of the Holy Spirit in the world could bring men and women outside the Church to a sense of their sin, to a sense of inadequacy before God, to a sense of dependence on God, to a sense of repentance. He gave many examples from the Muslim mystical tradition, in which he is an expert, to support the view that people could experience this kind of brokenness outside the boundaries of the Christian Church.

Such brokenness and repentance is not sufficient for salvation but it may be a preparation for it. Think of the figure of Cornelius in the Acts of the Apostles. I am sure that Cornelius was saved not because of his good works but because of his prayers to God. His dependence on God, his feeling that he was not worthy and that he needed God to save him: it was this that brought him to the gospel, to conversion and to baptism. And I am quite willing to see that people well outside the boundaries of the Church may be, indeed are, if the witness of the Bible is to be taken seriously, being prepared for God's revelation of himself to them.

Shall not the Judge Do Right?

Now when will such a revelation take place? When will they respond? Different answers have been given to these questions in the course of history.

The reformer Wycliffe, for example, thought that such people would be vouchsafed a vision of Christ on their deathbed and their response to such a vision would determine their eternal destiny. It is an interesting thought, though there is nothing in the Bible about it.[6]

Others say that such a revelation, if it does not occur in this life, can occur after death and they would refer you to the first Epistle of Peter, for example, where clearly the gospel is preached to rebellious people who did not hear God's Word at the time of Noah. There are two references in 1 Peter to this kind of preaching: in 1 Peter 3 and also in 1 Peter 4.[7]

Perhaps the best thing is for Christians to be positively agnostic, to say, look, we do not know what people's eternal destiny is, but we do know, because the Bible teaches us, that all people are being prepared for knowledge of God, that God is working in the histories and in the lives of all people and 'shall not the judge of all the earth do right?' (Gen. 18.25).

It is, perhaps, not possible for us to come to a definitive answer about this, except to say that what we know of God's mercy and forgiveness is that it is for all. And because we know that we are unworthy to receive this mercy and this forgiveness, we can also imagine God offering these to all.

In the end, the great visions in the Bible of people from many backgrounds, many tongues, many tribes, many nations, worshipping God must be what sustain us in our hope for humankind.[8]

'From the rising of the sun to its setting, my name is great among the nations, says the Lord.' (Mal. 1.11)

Notes

CHAPTER ONE

1. J. Goldingay, *Theological Diversity and the Authority of the Old Testament* (Grand Rapids, Mich., Eerdmans, 1987), pp. 29ff.
2. H. Wheeler Robinson, *The Religious Ideas of the Old Testament* (London, Duckworth, 1913), pp. 102ff.
3. D. Cohn-Sherbok, *On Earth as it is in Heaven: Jews, Christians and Liberation Theology* (Maryknoll, NY, Orbis, 1987).
4. J. V. Taylor, *The Go-Between God* (London, SCM Press, 1972), p. 17.
5. ibid., p. 44.
6. See further, L. Hodgson, *The Doctrine of the Trinity* (London, Nisbet, 1943), Lecture VI, pp. 144ff.
7. See M. Nazir-Ali, *Frontiers in Muslim–Christian Encounter* (Oxford, Regnum Books, 1987), pp. 15ff.
8. See further, H. Montefiore, *The Probability of God* (London, SCM Press, 1985).
9. B. W. Anderson, *The Living World of the Old Testament* (London, Longman, revised edn. 1978); K. A. Kitchen, *Ancient Orient and the Old Testament* (London, Tyndale Press, 1966), pp. 49, 69f.
10. N. K. Gottwald, *The Tribes of Yahweh: A Sociology of the Religion of Liberated Israel* (London, SCM Press, 1980), p. 611.
11. J. Goldingay, op. cit., p. 67.
12. See, for example, J. G. Baldwin, *Haggai, Zechariah and Malachi* (Tyndale Old Testament Commentaries, Leicester, Inter-Varsity Press, 1972), pp. 227ff.
13. O. Cullmann, *Christ and Time: The Primitive Conception of Time and History* (London, SCM Press, 1951), pp. 82, 117–118.
14. K. Barth, *Church Dogmatics* (Eng. tr., Edinburgh, T & T Clark, 1959), vol. 2, *The Doctrine of God*.
15. See G. Wainright (ed.), *Keeping the Faith: Essays to Mark the Centenary of 'Lux Mundi'* (London, SPCK, 1989); Robert Morgan (ed.), *The Religion of the Incarnation: Anglican Essays in Commemoration of 'Lux Mundi'* (Bristol, Bristol Classical Press, 1989).
16. C. Gore, *Dissertations on Subjects Connected with the Incarnation* (London, John Murray, 1895), pp. 69–226.
17. Charles Wesley, 'Come, O Thou Traveller unknown'.

CHAPTER TWO

1. Satirically named after Norman Tebbit, who advised unemployed young people to 'get on their bike' to find work.
2. L. Newbigin, *The Gospel in a Pluralist Society* (London, SPCK, 1989), p. 8off.

3. But see J. Baldwin, *Haggai, Zechariah and Malachi: An Introduction and Commentary* (London, Tyndale Press, 1972), pp. 224ff.
4. See the present writer's article in *Towards a Theology for Inter-Faith Dialogue* (London, ACC, 1986).
5. For an account of relations between Jews and Christians *before* the conversion of Constantine, see N. deLange, *Origen and the Jews: Studies in Jewish-Christian Relations in Third-Century Palestine* (Cambridge, CUP, 1976).
6. N. Saracco, 'The Liberating Options of Jesus' in V. Samuel and C. M. N. Sugden (eds.), *Sharing Jesus in the Two-Thirds World* (Bangalore, PIM, 1983), pp. 50ff.
7. For a recent discussion and criticism of Rahner's views, see M. Barnes SJ, *Religions in Conversation* (London, SPCK, 1989), p. 52ff.
8. See further, the present writer's 'Fidelity, Freedom and Friendship' in V. Samuel and A. Hauser (eds.), *Proclaiming Christ in Christ's Way* (Oxford, Regnum Books, 1989), pp. 85ff.
9. For an exposition and development of the Eastern position, see G. Khodr, 'Christianity in a Pluralist World – The Economy of the Holy Spirit' in C. G. Patelos, *The Orthodox Church in the Ecumenical Movement* (Geneva, WCC, 1978), pp. 297ff.
10. L. Newbigin, *The Gospel in a Pluralist Society* (London, SPCK, 1989).
11. ibid., pp. 52ff.
12. V. Donovan, *Christianity Rediscovered* (London, SCM Press, 1978).
13. *The Gospel in a Pluralist Society*, pp. 60f.
14. R. D. Laing, *The Facts of Life* (London, Penguin Books, 1977), p. 20.
15. L. Newbigin, op. cit., pp. 61ff and passim.
16. V. Samuel and A. Hauser (eds.), *Proclaiming Christ in Christ's Way*, pp. 221f.

CHAPTER THREE

1. C. Gore (ed.), *Lux Mundi: a series of studies in the religion of the Incarnation* (John Murray, 1889). For a review of its influence see R. Morgan (ed.), *The Religion of the Incarnation: Anglican Essays in Commemoration of 'Lux Mundi'* (Bristol, Bristol Classical Press, 1989).
2. Bede, *A History of the English Church and People*, translated and with an introduction by Leo Sherley-Price (Penguin Books, 1960), pp. 201ff, J. R. H. Moorman, *A History of the Church in England* (London, A & C Black, 1953).
3. Bede, pp. 83ff. M. Gallyon, *The early Church in Eastern England*, (Lavenham, Suffolk, Terence Dalton, 1973), pp. 28f.
4. 'Church, Culture and Change' in J. Draper (ed.), *Communion and Episcopacy* (Cuddesdon, 1988), pp. 99f.
5. D. W. Bebbington, *Evangelicalism in Modern Britain* (Unwin, London, 1989), pp. 229ff.
6. L. Boff, *Ecclesio-Genesis: The Base Communities Reinvent the Church* (London, Collins, 1986). See also *Transformation* July-Sept. 1986, Vol. 3, No. 3.
7. D. Gitari, 'Evangelisation and Culture: Primary Evangelism in Northern Kenya' in V. Samuel and A. Hauser (eds.), *Proclaiming Christ in Christ's Way*

(Regnum Books, Oxford, 1989), pp. 101ff. See also the Video *To Canterbury with a Camel* (CMS, 1990).

8. P. Price, *The Church as the Kingdom* (Basingstoke, Marshalls, 1987).

9. Charles Gore, for example. See further his *Dissertations on Subjects Connected with the Incarnation* (London, John Murray, 1895).

10. See further, M. Nazir-Ali, *From Everywhere to Everywhere* (London, Collins, 1990), pp. 149ff.

11. S. Sykes, 'An Anglican Theology of Evangelism' in *Theology*, Vol. XCIV, No. 762 Nov/Dec 91, pp. 405–414.

12. See further, I. H. Marshall, *The Gospel of Luke: A Commentary on the Greek Text* (Exeter, Paternoster Press, 1978), pp. 177ff.

13. *Isaiah 40—66* (London, SCM Press, 1969), pp. 366f.

14. M. Nazir-Ali, 'The Bible and Christian Witness' in *Using the Bible Today* (London, Bellew, 1991), pp. 170f.

15. See further, R. D. Sider, *The Gospel and its Proclamation: Message of the Fathers of the Church* (Delaware, Michael Glazier, 1983), chapters 2 and 3.

16. Pope John Paul II, *Redemptoris Missio: Encyclical on the Permanent Validity of the Church's Missionary Mandate*, Catholic International, Vol. 2 No. 6, March 1991 (Paris, Bayard-Presse), pp. 275f.

17. *De Incarnatione* (Oxford, Mowbrays, 1982), chapter V section 26ff.

18. R. D. Sider, op. cit., pp. 17ff.

19. L. Newbigin, *The Gospel in a Pluralist Society* (London, SPCK, 1989), p. 280.

20. R. D. Sider, op. cit., pp. 60ff, 104ff.

21. M. Assad, 'Mission in the Coptic Church', *Mission Studies*, Vol. IV: 1, 1987.

22. S. W. Sykes, op. cit.

23. R. D. Sider, op. cit., pp. 19, 105 and *passim*; M. Toal, *The Sunday Sermons of the Great Fathers* (London, Longman, 1963).

24. M. Nazir-Ali, *From Everywhere to Everywhere*, pp. 170. Elaine Storkey, *What's Right with Feminism* (London, SPCK, 1985).

25. See further, Nazir-Ali, op. cit., pp. 171f.

26. For a critical survey of contemporary *diakonia* see C. Ceccon and K. Paludan, *My Neighbour—Myself: Visions of Diakonia* (Geneva, WCC, 1988).

27. K. Y. Bock (ed.), *Minjung Theology: People as the Subjects of History* (Singapore, CCA, 1981); J. C. England, *Living Theology in Asia* (London, SCM, 1981), J. Massey, 'Christians in North India', *Religion and Society*, vol. XXXIV No. 3, 1987.

28. J. N. D. Anderson, *Christianity and World Religions: The Challenge of Pluralism* (Leicester, Inter-Varsity Press, 1980).

29. See further, J. Sobrino, *Christology at the Crossroads: a Latin American approach* (London, SCM Press, 1978).

30 Prudentius Aurelius Clemens: Latin poet and hymn-writer c. AD 350.

CHAPTER FOUR

1. W. H. Vanstone, *Love's Endeavour, Love's Expense: the response of being to the love of God* (London, Darton, Longman and Todd, 1977).

2. See further, R. Morgan, *The Religion of the Incarnation: Anglican Essays in Commemoration of 'Lux Mundi'* (Bristol, Bristol Classical Press, 1989).

3. L. Newbigin, *The Gospel in a Pluralist Society* (London, SPCK, 1989), pp. 198ff.
4. W. H. C. Frend, *The Early Church* (London, Hodder, 1965), pp. 119f and pp. 247ff.
5. See further, D. R. Winslow, 'Gregory Nazianzus and Love for the Poor', *Anglican Theological Review*, Oct. 1965, pp. 384ff; R. D. Sider, *The Gospel and Its Proclamation: Message of the Fathers of the Church* (Delaware, Michael Glazier, 1983).
6. D. W. Bebbington, *Evangelicalism in Modern Britain* (London, Unwin, 1989), pp. 69f, 121 etc.
7. E. Storkey, *What's Right with Feminism* (London, SPCK, 1985).
8. Charles Elliot's article is in J. Childress and J. Macquarrie (eds.), *A New Dictionary of Christian Ethics* (London, SCM Press, 1986).
9. R. D. N. Dickinson, *Poor, Yet Making Many Rich* (Geneva, WCC, 1983).

CHAPTER FIVE

1. See further, Paul Avis, *Anglicanism and the Christian Church* (T & T Clark, Edinburgh, 1989), pp. 24ff; V. J. K. Brook, *Archbishop Parker* (Oxford, OUP, 1962), pp. 322ff.
2. M. Nazir-Ali, *From Everywhere to Everywhere: A World View of Christian Mission* (London, Collins, 1990), pp. 38ff; G. Warneck, *Protestant Missions* (Edinburgh, 1906), pp. 8–9.
3. *Partners in Mission: Dublin 1973* (London, SPCK, 1973), pp. 53ff.
4. D. Bosch, *Transforming Mission* (Maryknoll, NY, Orbis, 1992).
5. C. Gore, *The Ministry of the Christian Church* (London, Rivingtons, 1889).
6. M. Nazir-Ali, op. cit., pp. 22ff.
7. J. D. Davies, *The Faith Abroad* (Oxford, Blackwell, 1983).
8. *Towards Dynamic Mission: Renewing the Church for Mission*, The Final Report, MISAG II (London, ACC, 1992), pp. 49ff. Also, *A Transforming Vision*, the Report of the Capetown meeting (London, CHP, 1993).
9. J. Bulloch, *The Life of the Celtic Church* (Edinburgh, 1963).
10. G. R. Evans and J. R. Wright (eds.), *The Anglican Tradition: A Handbook of Sources* (London, SPCK, 1991), pp. 78f.
11. J-M. Gaudeul, *Encounters and Clashes: Islam and Christianity in History* (Rome, Pontificio Istituto di Studi Arabi e Islamici, 1984), pp. 151ff.
12. M. Nazir-Ali, op. cit., p. 39 and pp. 139ff.
13. *For the Sake of the Kingdom: Report of the Inter-Anglican Theological and Doctrinal Commission* (London, ACC, 1986), pp. 38ff.
14. See further, A. Atiya, *Eastern Christianity* (London, Methuen, 1968).
15. In J. Childress and J. Macquarrie (eds.), *New Dictionary of Christian Ethics* (London, SCM Press, 1986), article on 'Economic Development', pp. 175ff.
16. M. Nazir-Ali, 'Dialogue in an Age of Conflict', in D. Cohn-Sherbok (ed.), *Many Mansions: Interfaith and Religious Intolerance* (London, Bellew, 1992), pp. 72 ff. See also G. Steiner, *Real Presences* (Cambridge, CUP, 1987) and J. Polkinghorne, *One World: Interaction of Science and Theology* (London, SPCK, 1986).

17. See E. J. Sharpe, 'The Goals of Inter-Religious Dialogue' in J. Hick (ed.), *Truth and Dialogue* (London, SPCK, 1974), pp. 77f. Also, *The Challenge of the Scriptures: the Bible and the Qur'ān* (Muslim-Christian Research Group, Maryknoll, NY, Orbis, 1989).

CHAPTER SIX

1. D. W. Bebbington, *Evangelicalism in Modern Britain* (London, Unwin, 1989).
2. J. Murray, *Proclaiming the Good News: A Short History of the CMS* (London, Hodder, 1985), pp. 11f.
3. See further, S. Neill, *A History of Christian Missions* (London, Penguin, 1964), p. 233.
4. J. H. Overton, *The Nonjurors* (London, 1902).
5. A. Mar Thoma, *The Mar Thoma Church: Heritage and Mission* (Tiruvalla, 1985).
6. H. Hill (ed.), *Light from the East* (Toronto, Anglican Book Centre, 1988).
7. A. J. van der Bent, *What in the World is the WCC?* (Geneva, World Council of Churches, 1991).
8. J. R. Wright (ed.), *Quadrilateral at One Hundred* (Cincinnati, Forward Movement Publications, 1988).
9. A. G. M. Stephenson, *Anglicanism and the Lambeth Conferences* (London, SPCK, 1978), pp. 128ff.
10. *Confessing the One Faith* (Faith and Order Paper No. 153, Geneva, World Council of Churches, 1991).
11. *Belonging Together* (a Document of the Inter-Anglican Theological and Doctrinal Consultation, London, ACC, 1992).
12. *Baptism, Eucharist and Ministry* (Geneva, World Council of Churches, 1982).
13. See further *The Final Report* of the Anglican–Roman Catholic International Commission (London, SPCK/CTS, 1982), *Authority in the Church I & II*.
14. *Baptism, Eucharist and Ministry*, pp. 2ff.
15. E. Schillebeeckx, *Christ the Sacrament* (London, SCM Press, 1963); J. Bowden, *Edward Schillebeeckx* (London, SCM Press, 1983).
16. For a general review of the ecumenical movement, see R. Rouse and S. C. Neill (eds.), *A History of the Ecumenical Movement 1517–1948* (London, SPCK, 1967).

CHAPTER SEVEN

1. G. Steiner, *Real Presences* (London, Faber, 1989).
2. R. D. Sider, *The Gospel and its Proclamation: Message of the Fathers of the Church* (Delaware, Michael Glazier, 1983), pp. 60ff. For a theological evaluation of the material in Justin and Clement, see K. Cracknell, *Towards a New Relationship: Christians and People of Other Faith* (London, Epworth, 1986, pp. 98ff).
3. It is, presumably, on passages such as these that the Augustinian and Reformation view of prevenient grace is based.

4. On the question of the diversity of the biblical material, as well as its underlying unity, see John Goldingay, *Theological Diversity and the Authority of the Old Testament* (Grand Rapids, Mich., Eerdmans, 1987).

5. W. Brueggemann, 'Trajectories in Old Testament Literature and the Sociology of Ancient Israel', *Journal of Biblical Literature*, 1979, No. 98, pp. 161–85.

6. See further, my 'Culture, Conversation and Conversion' in V. Samuel and C. M. N. Sugden (eds.), *AD 2000 and Beyond: a Mission Agenda* (Oxford, Regnum Books, 1991), p. 29.

7. N. Saracco, 'The Liberating Options of Jesus' in V. Samuel and C. M. N. Sugden (eds.), *Sharing Jesus in the Two-Thirds World* (Bangalore, PIM, 1983), pp. 49ff.

8. O. Kaiser, *Isaiah 1—12* (London, SCM Press, 1983), pp. 204f.

9. D. J. Sahas, *John of Damascus on Islam* (Leiden, Brill, 1972).

10. D. Hume, *Dialogues Concerning Natural Religion* in R. Wolheim (ed.), *Hume on Religion* (London, Fontana, 1963).

11. E. J. Sharpe, 'The Goals of Inter-Religious Dialogue' in J. Hick (ed.), *Truth and Dialogue* (London, SPCK, 1974), p. 77ff.

12. Pontifical Council for Inter-Religious Dialogue and the Congregation for the Evangelization of Peoples, *Dialogue and Proclamation*, reflection and orientation on Inter-Religious Dialogue and the proclamation of the Gospel of Jesus Christ. *The Bulletin*, issue 26/2, May 1991, p. 42f.

13. *The Challenge of the Scriptures: The Bible and the Qur'ān* (Maryknoll, NY, Orbis, 1989).

14. British Council of Churches, Committee for Relations with People of Other Faiths, *Relations with People of Other Faiths: Guidelines on Dialogue in Britain* (London, BCC, 1981).

15. See my *Islam: a Christian Perspective* (Exeter, Paternoster Press, 1983), p. 148. More recent documents continue to display this ambivalence. See report on CWME San Antonio Conference, F. R. Wilson (ed.), *The San Antonio Report, Your Will be Done: Mission in Christ's Way* (Geneva, World Council of Churches, 1990).

CHAPTER EIGHT

1. For a discussion see J. W. Sweetman, *Islam and Christian Theology*, Part II, Vol. II (London, Lutterworth, 1967), pp. 42ff.

2. M. Iqbal, *The Reconstruction of Religious Thought in Islam* (Lahore, Ashraf, 1971), pp. 181ff.

3. See, for example, R. Walzer, *Greek into Arabic* (Oxford, OUP, 1962).

4. M. Iqbal, *The Development of Metaphysics in Persia* (Lahore, Bazm-i-Iqbal, 1954), pp. 76ff. See also M. Smith, *Studies in Early Mysticism in the Near and Middle-East* (London, 1931).

5. H. A. R. Gibb and J. H. Kramers (eds.), *The Encyclopedia of Islam* (Leiden, E. J. Brill, 1974), articles *Fiqh* and *ᶜAda*.

6. S. Akhtar, *A Faith for all Seasons: Islam and Western Modernity* (London, Bellew, 1990); F. Rahman, *Islam and Modernity: Transformation of an Intellectual*

Tradition (Chicago, University of Chicago Press, 1982); A. Ahmad, *Postmodernism and Islam* (London, Routledge, 1992).

7. R. J. Rushdoony, *The Institutes of Biblical Law* (Phillipsburg, NJ, Presbyterian and Reformed, 1973). For a critique, see G. Fackre, *Ecumenical Faith in Evangelical Perspective* (Grand Rapids, Eerdmans, 1993).

8. S. Waliullah, *Hujjatullah Al Baligha*, Vol. 1 (Lahore, 1979), pp. 220f; cf. G. N. Jalbani, *The Teachings of Shah Waliullah* (Lahore, 1967), pp. 92f; M. Iqbal, *The Reconstruction*, pp. 171f.

9. See further, my *Islam: A Christian Perspective* (Exeter, Paternoster Press, 1983), pp. 48ff.

10. See further, Albert Hourani, *Arabic Thought in the Liberal Age* (Oxford, OUP, 1962); cf. A. Yusuf ᶜAli, *The Holy Qur'ān: Text, Translation and Commentary* (Leicester, Islamic Foundation, 1975), p. 111.

11. For the literature see Frank Clements, *The Emergence of Arab Nationalism: A Bibliography* (London, Diploma Press, 1976). See also K. Cragg, *The Arab Christian* (London, Mowbray, 1992).

12. In S. A. Vahid (ed.), *Islam as a Moral and Political Ideal: Thoughts, and Reflections of Iqbal* (Lahore, Ashraf, 1973), pp. 29ff.

13. *Islam: A Christian Perspective*, p. 117.

14. op. cit., p. 444, n.1270.

CHAPTER NINE

1. C. Padwick, *Muslim Devotions* (London, SPCK, 1961), p. 108.

2. A. H. Johns, *Prayer, Spirituality and Mysticism in Islam* (Rome, Encounter, 1983), p. 5.

3. *The Reconstruction of Religious Thought in Islam* (Lahore, Ashraf, 1971), p. 124.

4. M. Smith, *The Way of the Mystics* (London, Sheldon, 1976); M. Iqbal, *The Development of Metaphysics in Persia* (Lahore, Ashraf, 1964), pp. 76ff. See the present writer's *Islam: A Christian Perspective* (Exeter, Paternoster Press, 1983), pp. 60ff.

5. See, for example, Mahmud M. Ayub, *A Muslim Appreciation of Christian Holiness* (Rome, Encounter, 1987).

6. C. Padwick, op. cit., p. 92.

7. ibid., p. 219.

8. M. Smith, op. cit., pp. 125ff.

9. C. Padwick, op. cit., pp. 13ff.

10. T. Ware, *The Orthodox Church* (London, Penguin Books, 1973), pp. 74–5; cf. C. Padwick, op. cit., pp. 19f.

11. M. Iqbal, *The Reconstruction*, pp. 192f.

12. R. C. Zaehner, *Mysticism: Sacred and Profane* (Oxford, OUP, 1957) and *Concordant Discord* (Oxford, OUP, 1970).

13. M. Nazir-Ali, *Islam: A Christian Perspective*, pp. 65f.

14. See further, the present writer's *Frontiers in Muslim-Christian Encounter* (Oxford, Regnum Books, 1987), pp. 130ff.

15. M. Nazir-Ali, *Islam: A Christian Perspective*, pp. 84ff; Florence Antablin, 'Christian Buildings in Muslim Lands' (unpublished paper).

16. M. Nazir-Ali, *Frontiers*, pp. 77ff.

CHAPTER TEN

1. See further, J. T. Lienhard SJ, *Ministry: Message of the Fathers of the Church* (Delaware, Michael Glazier, 1984), pp. 36f; F. F. Bruce, *I and II Corinthians*, New Century Bible Commentary (Grand Rapids, Eerdmans, 1971), pp. 94f.
2. T. Shoji, 'The Church's Struggle for Freedom to Believe' in J. C. England (ed.), *Living Theology in Asia* (London, SCM Press, 1981), pp. 49ff.
3. C. F. D. Moule, *The Birth of the New Testament* (London, A & C Black, 1962), pp. 11ff.
4. See N. R. M. deLange, *Origen and the Jews: Studies in Jewish Christian Relations in Third Century Palestine* (Cambridge, CUP, 1976).
5. E.g., the Cathedral of St John the Baptist at Damascus. See my *Islam: A Christian Perspective* (Exeter, Paternoster Press, 1983), p. 37.
6. E. A. Pratt, *Can we Pray with the Unconverted?* (London, CPAS, 1971).
7. In an Islamic context, see my *Frontiers in Muslim-Christian Encounter* (Oxford, Regnum Books, 1987), pp. 15ff.
8. See further, *Multi-Faith Worship? Questions and Answers from the Inter-Faith Consultative Group* (London, CHP, 1992).

CHAPTER ELEVEN

1. H. Croner (ed.), *Stepping Stones to Further Jewish-Christian Relations* (New York, Stimulus, 1977), and *More Stepping Stones to Jewish-Christian Relations* (New York, Stimulus, 1985).
2. For discussions of the Holocaust's theological significance, see E. S. Fiorenza and D. Tracy (eds.), *The Holocaust as Event of Interruption* (Concilium 175, Edinburgh, 1984); A. A. Cohen, *The Tremendum* (New York, 1981); A. H. Friedlander, *The Death Camps and Theology within the Jewish-Christian Dialogue* (London, 1985).
3. Bat Ye'or, *The Dhimmi* (Cranbury, NJ; Associated University Presses, 1985).
4. See R. Walzer, *Greek into Arabic* (Oxford, OUP, 1962); O'Leary, *How Greek Science Passed to the Arabs* (London, deLacy, 1940).
5. S. S. Koder, *Kerala and the Jews* (Cochin, 1984).
6. M. H. Ellis, *Towards a Jewish Theology of Liberation* (London, SCM Press, 1987); N. Ateek, *Justice and Only Justice: A Palestinian Theology of Liberation* (Maryknoll, NY, Orbis, 1989).
7. A. Koestler, *The Thirteenth Tribe* (New York, Random House, 1976); N. R. M. deLange, *Origen and the Jews*. Cf. pp. 25 and 117.
8. C. Chapman, *Whose Promised Land?* (Tring, Lion Publishing, 1983).
9. *Nostra Aetate*, in A. Flannery (ed.), *The Documents of Vatican II* (New York, Costello, 1987), p. 738.
10. R. C. D. Jasper and G. J. Cuming, *Prayers of the Eucharist: Early and Reformed* (London, Collins, 1975), p. 9f.
11. M. J. Nazir-Ali and W. D. Pattinson (eds.), *The Truth Shall Make You Free: Report of the 1988 Lambeth Conference* (London, ACC, 1988), Appendix 6, pp. 299ff.
12. Paul Van Buren, *A Theology of Jewish-Christian Reality* (New York, Harper and

Row, 1988); *A Christian Theology of the People Israel* (New York, Harper and Row, 1988).

13. J. Jocz, *Jewish People and Jesus Christ* (London, SPCK, 1954).

CHAPTER TWELVE

1. R. Pannikar, *The Unknown Christ of Hinduism* (London, DLT, 1964), pp. 119ff.
2. K. Cragg, *The Mind of the Qur'ān* (London, Allen and Unwin, 1973), p. 44.
3. R. Pannikar, op. cit., p. 128.
4. K. Cragg, op. cit., pp. 38ff.
5. G. D'Costa, *Theology and Religions Pluralism* (Oxford, Blackwell, 1986), pp. 29ff.
6. J. A. T. Robinson, *Truth is Two-Eyed* (London, SCM Press, 1979), p. 129.
7. See further, M. Barnes, *Religious in Conversation: Christian Identity and Religious Pluralism* (London, SPCK, 1989), pp. 52ff.
8. R. D. Sider, *The Gospel and its Proclamation: Message of the Fathers of the Church* (Delaware, Michael Glazier, 1983), pp. 60ff.
9. J. N. D. Anderson, *God's Law and God's Love* (London, Collins, 1980), p. 128.
10. G. Khodr, 'Christianity in a Pluralistic World—the Economy of the Holy Spirit' in *The Orthodox Church in the Ecumenical Movement* (Geneva, WCC, 1978), pp. 297ff.
11. See further, my *Islam: A Christian Perspective* (Exeter, Paternoster Press, 1983) and *Frontiers in Muslim-Christian Encounter* (Oxford, Regnum Books, 1987). See also G. Basetti-Sani, *The Koran in the Light of Christ* (Chicago, Franciscan Press, 1977).
12. M. M. Thomas, *The Acknowledged Christ of the Indian Renaissance* (London, SCM Press, 1969).
13. See further, Polkinghorne's *Science and Creation: the Search for Understanding* (London, SPCK, 1990) and Davies, *The Mind of God: Scientific Basis for a Rational World* (London, Penguin Books, 1993).
14. S. Metcalf in *The Independent* 21 June 1993; cf George Steiner, *Real Presences* (London, Faber, 1989).
15. J. V. Taylor, *The Go-Between God* (London, SCM Press, 1972), p. 181.

CHAPTER THIRTEEN

1. W. J. Phythian-Adams, *The Call of Israel: An Introduction to the Study of Divine Election* (Oxford, OUP, 1934).
2. C. F. D. Moule, *The Origins of Christology* (Cambridge, CUP, 1977).
3. See further, J. R. W. Stott, *The Authentic Jesus* (London, Marshall Pickering, new edition, 1992); D. L. Edwards, *The Real Jesus* (London, Collins, 1992); N. T. Wright, *Who Was Jesus?* (London, SPCK, 1992).
4. R. Stannard, *Science and the Renewal of Belief* (London, SCM Press, 1982).
5. J. A. T. Robinson, *Wrestling with Romans* (London, SCM Press, 1979).
6. See further, R. W. Southern, *Western Views of Islam in the Middle Ages*

(Cambridge, Mass., 1962); J. M. Gaudeul, *Encounters and Clashes*, vol. 1 (Rome, Pontifical Institute for Arabic and Islamic Studies, 1984), pp. 131ff.

7. C. Bigg, *St Peter and St Jude* (Edinburgh, T & T Clark, 1987), pp. 162ff, 170f.
8. D. L. Edwards and J. R. W. Stott, *Essentials* (London, Hodder & Stoughton, 1988).

Select Bibliography

Liberation and Contexual Theologies

N. Ateek, *Justice and Only Justice: A Palestinian Theology of Liberation* (Maryknoll, NY; Orbis, 1989).

K. Y. Bock (ed.), *Minjing Theology: People as the Subjects of History* (Singapore, CCA, 1981).

L. Boff, *Ecclesio-Genesis: The Base Communities Reinvent the Church* (London, Collins, 1986).

C. Chapman, *Whose Promised Land?* (Tring, Lion Publishing, 1983).

D. Cohn-Sherbok, *On Earth as it is in Heaven: Jews, Christians and Liberation Theology* (Maryknoll, NY; Orbis, 1987).

M. Ellis, *Towards a Jewish Theology of Liberation* (London, SCM Press, 1987).

J. C. England, *Living Theology in Asia* (London, SCM Press, 1981).

P. Price, *The Church as the Kingdom* (Basingstoke, Marshalls, 1987).

V. K. Samuel and C.M.N. Sudgen (eds.), *Sharing Jesus in the Two-Thirds World* (Bangalore, PIM, 1983).

E. Storkey, *What's Right with Feminism* (London, SPCK, 1985).

Christian Doctrine

Athanasius, *De Incarnatione* (Oxford, Mowbray, 1982).

K. Barth, *Church Dogmatics* (Eng. trans., Edinburgh, T & T Clark, 1959).

O. Cullmann, *Christ and Time: The Primitive Conception of Time and History* (London, SCM Press, 1951).

D. L. Edwards and J. R. W. Stott, *Essentials* (London, Hodder and Stoughton, 1988).

C. Gore, *The Ministry of the Christian Church* (London, Rivingtons, 1889).

L. Hodgson, *The Doctrine of the Trinity* (London, Nisbet, 1943).

J. T. Lienhard, SJ, *Ministry: Message of the Fathers of the Church* (Delaware, Michael Glazier, 1984).

E. Schillebeeckx, *Christ the Sacrament* (London, SCM Press, 1963).

J. Sobrino, *Christology at the Crossroads: A Latin American Approach* (London, SCM Press, 1972).

J. V. Taylor, *The Go-Between God* (London, SCM Press, 1972).

W. H. Vanstone, *Love's Endeavour, Love's Expense: The Response of Being to the Love of God* (London, DLT, 1977).

Relations with People of Other Faiths

A. Ahmad, *Postmodernism and Islam* (London, Routledge, 1992).

S. Akhtar, *A Faith for All Seasons: Islam and Western Modernity* (London, Bellew, 1990).

J. N. D. Anderson, *Christianity and World Religions: The Challenge of Pluralism* (Leicester, Inter-Varsity Press, 1980).

J. N. D. Anderson, *God's Law and God's Love* (London, Collins, 1980).

M. Barnes, *Religions in Conversation* (London, SPCK, 1989).

Bat Ye'or, *The Dhimmi* (Cranbury, NJ; Associated University Presses, 1985).

G. Basetti-Sani, *The Koran in the Light of Christ* (Chicago, Franciscan Press, 1977).

D. Cohn-Sherbok, *Many Mansions: Interfaith and Religious Intolerance* (London, Bellew, 1992).

K. Cracknell, *Towards a New Relationship: Christians and People of Other Faith* (London, Epworth, 1986).

K. Cragg, *The Mind of the Qur'an* (London, Allen and Unwin, 1973).

H. Croner (ed.), *Stepping Stones to Further Jewish-Christian Relations* (New York, Stimulus, 1977) and *More Stepping Stones to Jewish-Christian Relations* (New York, Stimulus, 1988).

G. D'Costa, *Theology and Religious Pluralism* (Oxford, Blackwell, 1986).

N. deLange, *Origen and the Jews: Studies in Jewish-Christian Relations in Third-Century Palestine* (Cambridge, CUP, 1976).

J. M. Gaudeul, *Encounters and Clashes: Islam and Christianity in History* (Rome, Pontificio Istituto di Studi Arabi e Islamici, 1984).

J. Hick (ed.), *Truth and Dialogue* (London, SPCK, 1974).

M. Iqbal, *The Reconstruction of Religious Thought in Islam* (Lahore, Ashraf, 1971).

M. Iqbal, *The Development of Metaphysics in Persia* (Lahore, Bazm-i-Iqbal, 1954).

G. N. Jalbani, *The Teachings of Shah Waliullah* (Lahore, 1967).

J. Jocz, *Jewish People and Jesus Christ* (London, SPCK, 1954).

A. Koestler, *The Thirteenth Tribe* (New York, Random House, 1976).

M. Nazir-Ali, *Islam: A Christian Perspective* (Exeter, Paternoster Press, 1983).

N. Nazir-Ali, *Frontiers in Muslim-Christian Encounter* (Oxford, Regnum Books, 1987).

C. Padwick, *Muslim Devotions* (London, SPCK, 1961).

R. Pannikar, *The Unknown Christ of Hinduism* (London, DLT, 1964).

F. Rahman, *Islam and Modernity: Transformation of an Intellectual Tradition* (University of Chicago Press, 1982).

J. A. T. Robinson, *Truth is Two-Eyed* (London, SCM Press, 1979).

D. J. Sahas, *John of Damascus on Islam* (Leiden, Brill, 1972).

M. Smith, *Studies in Early Mysticism in the Near and Middle-East* (London, 1931).

R. W. Southern, *Western Views of Islam in the Middle Ages* (Cambridge, Mass., 1962).

J. W. Sweetman, *Islam and Christian Theology* (Lutterworth, London, 1967).

M. M. Thomas, *The Acknowledged Christ of the Hindu Renaissance* (London, SCM Press, 1969).

P. Van Buren, *A Theology of Jewish-Christian Reality* (New York, Harper and Row, 1988) and *A Theology of the People Israel* (New York, Harper and Row, 1988).

R. C. Zaehner, *Mysticism: Sacred and Profane* (Oxford, OUP, 1957).

R. C. Zaehner, *Concordant Discord* (Oxford, OUP, 1970).

Dialogue and Proclamation, Pontifical Council for Inter-Religious Dialogue and the Congregation for the Evangelization of Peoples, *The Bulletin* (Issue 26/2, May 1991).

Multi-Faith Worship? Questions and Answers from the Inter-Faith Consultative Group (London, CHP, 1992).

Relations with People of Other Faiths: Guidelines on Dialogue in Britain (London, BBC, 1981).

The Challenge of the Scriptures: The Bible and the Qu'rān, Muslim-Christian Research Group (Maryknoll, NY; Orbis, 1989).

Art and Literature

R. Etchells, *A Model of Making* (Basingstoke, Marshall, Morgan and Scott, 1982).

G. Steiner, *Real Presences* (Cambridge, CUP, 1987).

M. Takenaka and R. O'Grady, *The Bible Through Arian Eyes* (Auckland, N.Z.; Pace, 1991).

F. Willett, *African Art* (London, Thames and Hudson, 1971).

Apologetics

P. Davies, *The Mind of God: Scientific Basis for a Rational World* (London, Penguin Books, 1993).

H. Montefiore, *The Probability of God* (London, SCM Press, 1985).

L. Newbigin, *The Gospel in a Pluralist Society* (London, SPCK, 1989).

A. Peacocke, *Theology for a Scientific Age* (London, SCM Press, 1993).

J. Polkinghorne, *One World: Interaction of Science and Theology* (London, SPCK, 1986).

J. Polkinghorne, *Science and Creation: The Search for Understanding* (London, SPCK, 1990).

R. Stannard, *Science and the Renewal of Belief* (London, SCM Press, 1982).

Theology of Mission

V. Donovan, *Christianity Rediscovered: An Epistle from the Masai* (London, SCM Press, 1978).

H. H. John Paul II, *Redemptoris Missio: Encyclical on the Permanent Validity of the Church's Missionary Mandate*, Catholic International, Vol. 2 No. 6 (Paris, Bayard-Presse, 1991).

M. Nazir-Ali, *From Everywhere to Everywhere: A World View of Christian Mission* (London, Collins, 1990).

V. K. Samuel and A. Hauser (eds.), *Proclaiming Christ in Christ's Way* (Oxford, Regnum Books, 1989).

R. D. Sider, *The Gospel and its Proclamation: Message of the Fathers of the Church* (Delaware, Michael Glazier, 1983).

Your Will Be Done: Mission in Christ's Way, Report of the San Antonio Conference of Commission on World Mission and Evangelism (Geneva, WCC, 1990).

Biblical Material

B. W. Anderson, *The Living World of the Old Testament* (London, Longman, rev. edn, 1978).

W. Brueggemann, *The Land: Place as Gift, Promise and Challenge in Biblical Faith* (London, SPCK, 1978).

J. Goldingay, *Theological Diversity and the Authority of the Old Testament* (Grand Rapids, MI; Eerdmans, 1987).

N. K. Gottwald, *The Tribes of Yahweh: A Sociology of the Religion of Liberated Israel* (London, SCM Press, 1980).

K. A. Kitchen, *Ancient Orient and the Old Testament* (London, Tyndale Press, 1966).

C. F. D. Moule, *The Birth of the New Testament* (London A & C Black, 1962).

C. F. D. Moule, *The Origins of Christology* (Cambridge, CUP, 1977).

W. J. Phythian-Adams, *The Call of Israel: An Introduction to the Study of Divine Election* (Oxford, OUP, 1934).

J. A. T. Robinson, *Wrestling with Romans* (London, SCM Press, 1979).

J. R. W. Stott, *The Authentic Jesus* (London, Marshall Pickering, new edn, 1992); D. L. Edwards, *The Real Jesus* (London, Collins, 1992); N. T. Wright, *Who Was Jesus?* (London, SPCK, 1992).

H. Wheeler Robinson, *The Religious Ideas of the Old Testament* (London, Duckworth, 1913).

Ecumenism

C. Ceccon and K. Paludan (eds.), *My Neighbour—Myself: Visions of Diakonia* (Geneva, WCC, 1988).

G. Fackre, *Ecumenical Faith in Evangelical Perspective* (Grand Rapids, MI; Eerdmans, 1993).

A. Flannery (ed.), *The Documents of Vatican II* (New York, Costello, 1987).

H. Hill (ed.), *Light from the East* (Toronto, Anglican Book Centre, 1988).

R. Rouse and S. C. Neill (eds.), *A History of the Ecumenical Movement 1517–1948* (London, SPCK, 1967).

A. J. VanderBent, *What in the World is the WCC?* (Geneva, WCC, 1991).

T. Ware, *The Orthodox Church* (London, Penguin Books, 1973).

Confessing the One Faith, Faith and Order Paper 153 (Geneva, WCC, 1991).

Baptism Eucharist and Ministry (Geneva, WCC, 1982).

The Final Report: ARCIC (London, CTS/SPCK, 1982).

C. G. Patelos (ed.), *The Orthodox Church in the Ecumenical Movement* (Geneva, WCC, 1978).

Development

D. Abecassis, *Identity, Islam and Human Development in Rural Bangladesh* (Dhaka, University Press, 1990).

R. D. N. Dickinson, *Poor, yet Making Many Rich* (Geneva, WCC, 1983).

V. Mangalwadi, *Truth and Social Reform* (Delhi, Nivedit, 1989).

V. K. Samuel and C. M. N. Sugden (eds.), *The Church in Response to Human Need* (Grand Rapids, MI; Eerdmans, 1987).

The Gospel, the Poor and the Churches (London, Christian Aid, 1994).

Philosophy

A. Hourani, *Arabic Thought in the Liberal Age* (Oxford, OUP, 1962).
R. Wolheim, *Hume on Religion* (London, Fontana, 1963).

Anglicanism

Paul Avis, *Anglicanism and the Christian Church* (Edinburgh, T & T Clark, 1989).
G. R. Evans and J. R. Wright (eds.), *The Anglican Tradition: A Handbook of Sources* (London, SPCK, 1991).
R. Morgan (ed.), *The Religion of the Incarnation: Anglican Essays in Commemoration of 'Lux Mundi'* (Bristol, Bristol Classical Press, 1989).
M. Nazir-Ali and W. D. Pattinson (eds.), *The Truth Shall Make You Free: Report of the 1988 Lambeth Conference* (London, ACC, 1988).
J. H. Overton, *The Nonjurors* (London, 1902).
A. G. M. Stephenson, *Anglicanism and the Lambeth Conferences* (London, SPCK, 1978).
G. Wainwright (ed.), *Keeping The Faith: Essays to Mark the Centenary of 'Lux Mundi'* (London, SPCK, 1989).
J. R. Wright (ed.), *Quadrilateral at One Hundred* (Cincinnati Forward Movement, 1988).
Belonging Together, Inter-Anglican Theological and Doctrinal Consultation (London, ACC, 1992).
For the Sake of the Kingdom: Report of the Inter-Anglican Theological and Doctrinal Commission (London, ACC, 1986).

Mission and Church History

A. Atiya, *Eastern Christianity* (London, Methuen, 1968).
D. W. Bebbington, *Evangelicalism in Modern Britain* (London, Unwin, 1989).
Bede, *A History of the English Church and People*, trans. with an intro. by L. Sherley-Price (London, Penguin Books, 1960).
K. Cragg, *The Arab Christian* (London, Mowbray, 1992).
J. D. Davies, *The Faith Abroad* (Oxford, Blackwell, 1983).
W. H. C. Frend, *The Early Church* (London, Hodder and Stoughton, 1965).
A. Mar Thoma, *The Mar Thoma Church: Heritage and Mission* (Tiruvalla, 1985).
J. R. H. Moorman, *A History of the Church in England* (London, A & C Black, 1953).
J. Murray, *Proclaiming the Good News: A Short History of the Church Missionary Society* (London, Hodder and Stoughton, 1985).
S. Neill, *A History of Christian Missions* (London, Penguin Books, 1964).
G. Warneck, *Protestant Missions* (Edinburgh, 1906).

Index of Names and Subjects

Index of Qur'ānic References

Index of Biblical References